The End of the
Ancient Republic

The End of the Ancient Republic
Shakespeare's *Julius Caesar*

Jan H. Blits

ROWMAN & LITTLEFIELD PUBLISHERS, INC.

ROWMAN & LITTLEFIELD PUBLISHERS, INC.

Published in the United States of America
by Rowman & Littlefield Publishers, Inc.
4720 Boston Way, Lanham, Maryland 20706

British Cataloging in Publication Information Available

Library of Congress Cataloging-in-Publication Data

Blits, Jan H.
The end of the ancient republic : Shakespeare's Julius
Caesar / Jan H. Blits.
p.   cm.
Originally published: Durham, N.C. : Carolina Academic
Press, © 1982.
Includes index.
1. Shakespeare, William, 1564–1616. Julius Caesar.
2. Caesar, Julius, in fiction, drama, poetry, etc.
3. Political plays, English—History and criticism.
4. Rome in literature.   I. Title.
PR2808.B55   1992
822.3'3—dc20   92–13744 CIP

ISBN 0–8476–7760–5 (pbk. : alk. paper)

Printed in the United States of America

 ™ The paper used in this publication meets the minimum requirements of
American National Standard for Information Sciences—Permanence of
Paper for Printed Library Materials, ANSI Z39.48–1984.

For Kathleen

Preface

THESE ESSAYS OFFER AN INTERPRETATION OF *JULIUS CAESAR*, SHAKESPEARE'S study of the end of the Roman Republic and the rise of the political phenomenon known today as Caesarism. Republican Rome rested on two related conditions—internecine war between the city's nobles and common people and external war between Rome and the world beyond her borders. But as Rome's domestic strife allowed or perhaps compelled her to conquer the world, so universal empire ended her faction and, with it, the Republic itself. Having conquered the world, Rome succumbed to her own conquering hero. As *Caesar* shows, Rome's new Caesarian regime is characterized by the liberation of private concerns and the ascendancy of personal loyalty, and is distinguished from other forms of despotism largely by its origins. Arising from a decline of public spirit and civic virtue, it stems from a free and prosperous people's voluntary surrender of their liberty rather than from a tyrant's violent seizure of power through revolution. Caesarism is inherent to the corruption of political life which destroyed republican Rome. Yet Shakespeare also shows that the vice of Caesarism—above all, its spirit of "personalism"—is, paradoxically, inherent to the republican regime as well. While more obviously characteristic of the Empire, it is nonetheless intrinsic to the Republic but suppressed or redirected to the public good by the city's wars and dissension. In this (as in virtually every other important respect) warlike Rome is defined chiefly by opposition. Honoring, as it does, manliness, war and conquest, it proves to be essentially akin to what it spiritedly opposes. While the Republic's leading defenders "all stand up against the spirit of Caesar," "Caesar's spirit" is what truly animates the "Soul of Rome" (II.i.167, 169, 321). Caesarism, in every sense the true end or consummation of the Roman Republic, is at once its destruction and its fulfillment—its final degradation and its ultimate completion.

I am grateful to the late Howard B. White for his early encouragement of my study of Shakespeare. I especially wish to thank Mera and Harvey Flaumenhaft for their helpful criticism of early drafts of most of these essays, and my wife, Kathleen Mazzie Blits, for the benefit of her excellent judgment and invaluable editorial assistance.

Chapter one originally appeared in a slightly different form in *Interpretation*, Vol. 9, No. 2, 3 (1981), and chapter two in *The Journal of Politics*, Vol. 43, No. 1 (Feb. 1981). I wish to thank the editors of those journals for permission to reprint.

All quotations are from the Arden edition of *Julius Caesar*, ed. T. S. Dorsch (London: Methuen, 1964) and the Kittredge editions of *Coriolanus* and *Antony and Cleopatra*, ed. George Lyman Kittredge, rev. Irving Ribner (New York: John Wiley and Sons, 1967, 1966).

One

Manliness and Friendship in *Julius Caesar*

> The city of Rome had besides its proper name another secret
> one, known only to a few. It is believed by some to have
> been "Valentia," the Latin translation of "Roma" ["strength"
> in Greek]; others think it was "Amor" ("Roma" read
> backwards).
>
> —G.W. F. Hegel, *The Philosophy of History.*

SHAKESPEARE'S *JULIUS CAESAR* EXAMINES THE LIVES AND SOULS OF THE
sort of men who made republican Rome the foremost model of
political greatness and glory. The men we see in the play have the
strongest desire for worldly glory and, regarding honor as the
highest good, relentlessly strive to win it. They look up to the
things that make men strong and, having tremendous pride and
trust in their own "strength of spirit" (I.iii.95), jealously contend
with one another for outstanding distinctions. Their hearts are, as
Cassius says, "hearts of controversy" (I.ii.108). Loving victory,
dominance and honor, they characteristically equate manliness
and human excellence. Cassius sums up their view of their humanity when, bemoaning Rome's acquiescence to Caesar, he says,

4 / The End of the Ancient Republic

> But, woe the while! our fathers' minds are dead,
> And we are govern'd with our mothers' spirits;
> Our yoke and sufferance show us womanish.
> (I.iii.82–84)

Rome is a man's world. No one in *Caesar* has a good word for women. Even Portia, Brutus' noble wife, is a misogynist. Even she, ashamed of her woman's heart, insists that the best human qualities neither come from nor belong to women.[1] If a woman like herself happens to show them, she does so in spite of her sex. She is "stronger than [her] sex" (II.i.296); she is manly.

That a woman must somehow overcome her nature to show the highest virtue points to the close correlation in *Caesar* between manliness and rising up or rising above the common or merely human things. Throughout the play men's activities and ambitions are repeatedly expressed in terms of standing, rising, climbing to new heights, "soar[ing] above the view of men" (I.i.74), and reaching "the upmost round" (II.i.24) while scorning everything below; and their defects and defeats expressed in the contrary terms of bending, bowing, lying, crouching, fawning, falling, sinking, kneeling, shaking, trembling, and melting.[2] The manly is associated with the firm, the brilliant, the cold, the independent, the high and the noble; the womanish, with the soft, the dull, the warm, the dependent, the low and the lowly. The manly is the outstanding; the womanish, the obscure. The manly both contains and confers distinctions. The womanish does neither. Like the body, it is the great equalizer. It tends to level all important differences.[3]

Shakespeare shows that the manly love of distinction engenders a characteristic attitude toward the world. It is one of resisting and overcoming all the things that threaten to drag a man down or

---

1. II.i.292ff.; II.iv.6–9, 39–40. For the Roman patriots' disparaging their maternal origins as much as they revere their paternal origins, see I.ii.111–114, 156–159; I.iii.80–84; II.i.294–297; IV.iii.118–122; V.iii.67–71; V.iv.1–11. Note also that "ancestor(s)" always refers only to men: I.ii.111, I.iii.80–84, II.i.53–54, III.ii.51. For the fact that "virtue" derives from the Latin word for "man," see Cicero, *Tusculan Disputations,* II.43.

2. E.g., I.i.72–75; I.ii.99–136; II.i.21–27, 118, 142, 167; III.i.31–77, 122–137, 148–150, 204–210; IV.ii.23–27; IV.iii.38–50, 66–69; V.i.41–44; V.iii.57–64.

3. I.ii.268–272; I.iii.80–84; II.i.122, 292–297; II.iv.6–10, 39–40.

overshadow him. This fundamental Roman stance is reflected in part by the great importance attached to wakefulness. Early on the ides of March, Brutus tells the other conspirators that he has been "awake all night" (II.i.88). Indeed,

> Since Cassius first did whet me against Caesar,
> I have not slept.
> (61–62)

His servant, Lucius, can "Enjoy the honey-heavy dew of slumber," because, as Brutus says, the boy has none of the "busy care[s]" that occupy "the brains of men" (230,232). But the conspirators and Caesar alike have been kept awake by just such cares. Only those outside the political realm belong in bed. Thus Brutus sends Lucius back to bed soon after awakening him and, shortly afterwards, tells Portia, too, to "go to bed" when she complains of his having left "his wholesome bed" (237ff.). But he himself is aroused to act against Caesar by Cassius' anonymous note accusing him of sleeping and urging him to awake (46ff.); and then, arguing that they need nothing but their Roman cause to "prick" them to action, he spurs his co-conspirators on by associating "The melting spirits of women"—in contrast to "th' insuppressive mettle of our spirits"—with each man returning "to his idle bed" (114ff.).[4] It is not going too far to say that from the Roman point of view nothing very interesting ever happens in bed.[5]

Brutus and the others understand the private world to be destructive of manliness. As he indicates at Sardis shortly before the decisive battle of Philippi, to succumb to sleep is to succumb to necessity. Brutus finally puts his work aside and prepares for bed only because "nature must obey necessity" (IV.iii.226). Natural necessity, he implies, is not part of his nature. His noble nature is to oppose

---

4. See also I.iii.164, II.i.98–99; and cf. in context IV.iii. 92ff. For Lucius, see further IV.iii.235–271. And for Caesar's estimation of "such men as sleep a-nights," see I.ii.189f. Also, note II.ii.116–117.

5. Just as the possibility of a Roman woman warrior like Antony's wife Fulvia is totally suppressed in *Caesar* (see *A&C*, I.i.81–87; II.i.40; II.ii.42–44, 61–66, 94–98; also I.i.20, 28–32; I.ii.100ff.), so too is Caesar's erotic interest in a woman like Cleopatra (see *ibid* I.v.29–31, 66–75; II.ii.226–228; II.vi.64–70; III.xiii.116–117; cp. *JC*, I.ii.1–11.

necessity. So while women and children "look for a time of rest" (261), Brutus "will niggard" sleep with only "a little rest" (227). He opposes "murd'rous slumber" (266) because he opposes any form of obscurity. Men like him resist all forms of reclining because to recline is to surrender one's standing in the world. Their characteristic opposition to the earth's downward pull is well expressed by Alexander the Great's remark that, more than anything else, sleep and sex reminded him he was not a god.[6]

The specific character of manly virtue is indicated by Portia, who gashes herself in the thigh to prove that she is strong enough to keep Brutus' secret plans in confidence. The important difference between the sexes, she seems to believe, is that men are stronger than their bodies but women are not. Women are inconstant because they are weaker than bodily fears and pains.[7] One might therefore suppose that their characteristic trait is concern with necessary rather than with noble things. But Portia's subsequent actions reveal something she herself fails to see. The self-inflicted wound she calls "strong proof of my constancy" (II.i.299) turns out to be no proof at all. As soon as Brutus leaves, she is overwhelmed by anxious fears for his welfare, and her strong "patience" (301) and manly endurance quickly vanish. There are evidently worse tortures for her than bodily pains and even death. Love for her husband makes her more a woman than the superiority to her body makes her a man. If, as she says, "The heart of woman" is a "weak thing" (II.iv.39–40), her actions seem to show its weakness stems not from fear but from affection, from loving another not from loving oneself.

While manliness no doubt sustains a timocracy like the Roman Republic, such an honor-loving regime is often praised for fostering fraternity. Its citizens, bound together by a common ancestry and upbringing, are free and equal; they respect the mutual claims

---

6. Plutarch, *Alexander the Great*, 22.3.
7. For the importance of constancy, see esp. Caesar's claim to heroic divinity at III.i.31–77, esp. 58–73.

to rule that only manly virtue can enforce. It is therefore fitting that only "man" is mentioned in *Caesar* more often than "love" or "friendship"[8] and the most elaborated friendship in the play is that of the leaders of the republican faction. In fact, Brutus and Cassius call each other "brother" as many as eight times[9] although Shakespeare never explains that they are brothers-in-law.[10] Shakespeare's silence is appropriately misleading. Brutus and Cassius' fraternal form of address seems entirely elective and a sign of the sort of friendship nurtured by the manly regime under which they live and which they die defending.[11] Their friendship does, I think, epitomize the Republic, but not as just suggested or usually understood.

The implications of the Roman view of virtue are strikingly revealed when the tensions inherent in Brutus and Cassius' friendship surface in their ugly quarrel at Sardis late in the play. Indeed, manliness and friendship are the express themes of the quarrel. Two principal threads, closely tied, run through the scene: 1) presuming upon Cassius' expressed love, Brutus challenges his manliness and, in particular, demeans and taunts his proud anger (esp. IV.iii.38–50); and 2) he refuses to confess any love until Cassius shames himself by announcing that he utterly despairs of Brutus' contempt and will do anything to have his love (92–106). What is perhaps most telling, however, occurs not during the quarrel itself but during their apparent reconciliation (106ff.). Cassius' previous conciliatory efforts notwithstanding, Brutus still makes him solicit an explicit admission of love and forces him to plead for it, moreover, by accepting Brutus' degrading characterization of his anger as the effect of an irritable, unmanly disposition (39–50, 106–112). Thus Cassius, apologizing for having gotten angry in the first place, diffidently asks,

---

8. "Man" (including its variants) appears 148 times; "love," 51 times; "friend," 53 times. By comparison, "Rome" occurs 38, "Roman" and "Romans" together 35 times. Only Caesar's name is mentioned more often than "man."

9. IV.ii.37, 39; IV.iii.95, 211, 232, 236, 247, 303; see also II.i.70.

10. See Plutarch, *Brutus*, 6.1–2.

11. Shakespeare's silence also has the effect of concealing that Cassius is married, thus making him appear a fully spirited or public man.

> Have not you love enough to bear with me,
> When that rash humour which my mother gave me
> Makes me forgetful?

And Brutus answers with only a meager "Yes," to which he quickly adds, sealing Cassius' disgrace,

> . . . and from henceforth
> When you are over-earnest with your Brutus,
> He'll think your mother chides, and leave you so.
> (118–122)

Brutus confesses only to having enough love to overlook Cassius' womanish spirit. He shall excuse his "over-earnestness" because he shall regard such fits of temper as the chiding of Cassius' mother rather than the spirited anger proper to a man.

Men such as Brutus are ambitious for love. They wish to be loved rather than to love because being loved closely resembles being honored.[12] Both are tributes of esteem. Love between such men is therefore jealous; like honor, it is ardently sought and only begrudgingly given. Unrequited "shows of love" (I.ii.33,46) therefore amount to confessions of envy. A Roman, moreover, is a man's man. He admires manly men and seeks love from men he himself could love. The erotic Antony is disparaged by his own men in *Antony and Cleopatra* not simply because he flees battle to pursue Cleopatra, but, more generally, because he fights bravely chiefly to impress a woman and win her love. As one of his officers complains, "so our leader's led, / And we are women's men" (III.vii,69–70). The republican contest for love, however, is a contest in manliness for the love of other manly men. Moments before the quarrel, Brutus, anticipating the heart of the quarrel, contrasts true and false friends. The difference turns wholly on manly strength. Using a metaphor from war to describe what constitutes a false friend, he says,

---

12. Aristotle, *Nicomachean Ethics,* 1159a13–15.

> But hollow men, like horses hot at hand,
> Make gallant show and promise of their mettle;
> But when they should endure the bloody spur,
> They fall their crests, and like deceitful jades
> Sink in the trial.
> (IV.ii.23–27)

False friends are hollow warriors. They lack the dauntless strength they pretend to have. The quarrel brings out the significance of this view of virtue and friendship: the manly contest for love issues finally in a struggle to crush a friend by unmanning his proud heart. Love is not an end in itself, but rather a means to win victory in the defeat and shame of a friend.[13]

Manliness is a contentious virtue. It is a "virtue" that "cannot live / Out of the teeth of emulation" (II.iii.11–12). Untempered, it is hungry, devouring, and finally self-consuming. Nothing could lower Cassius more in Brutus' esteem than his swallowing his repeated abuse and openly confessing that he is "Hated by one he loves; brav'd by his brother" (IV.iii.95). But manly love is spirited, not affectionate. It does not aim at collapsing the distance between men into intimacy but rather at expanding that distance to the point where friendship finally becomes impossible, as Caesar himself most vividly demonstrates. As manliness is displayed primarily in battle, so the combat between warriors does not stop at the city's walls. It pervades their loves as well as their enmities. Rome's civil strife seems to be Roman friendship writ large.

Antony, the major counterexample, is in many ways the exception who confirms the rule. No one can doubt that his love is spirited and has an ambitious quality. But his sought-for victory in love is altogether different from Brutus'. Just as he declares at the outset of *Antony and Cleopatra* that the "nobleness of life" is for lovers to embrace

> . . . when such a mutual pair
> And such a twain can do't, in which I bind,

---

13. See esp. IV.iii.41–50.

> On pain of punishment, the world to weet
> We stand up peerless,
> (I.i.36–40)

so too, when he thinks Cleopatra has killed herself for him, he wishes to end his own life so that, reunited in death, they can win even greater acknowledgment as a matchless pair:

> Eros!—I come, my queen.—Eros!—Stay for me.
> Where souls do couch on flowers, we'll hand in hand
> And with our sprightly port make the ghosts gaze.
> Dido and her Aeneas shall want troops,
> And all the haunt be ours.
> (IV.xiv.50–54)[14]

Antony wants to out-love all other great lovers and be recognized as the greatest lover the world has ever known. The achievement he imagines may imply the defeat of all other heroic lovers, but his victory would in no sense be the defeat of his own lover. He does not seek to win another's "hot" love (*JC*,IV.ii.19) while coldly withholding his own. On the contrary, his envisaged triumph is shared by Cleopatra and is, moreover, their shared glory as a singular couple. Indeed, it rests on the wished-for prospect that nothing at all, not even their bodies, will ever again separate their souls. It is the victory of the utmost devotion and intimacy between "a mutual pair".

Antony neither resents Caesar's domination like Cassius, nor seeks to dominate other men's hearts like Brutus. Yet, while having great love for Caesar, he never presumes an equality with him. His ready submission may therefore seem to foreshadow the Empire where the Emperor has no equals and all citizens are reduced to private men subject to his will.[15] But Antony loves Caesar solely for his superlative nobility and not for his favors. To him, Caesar

---

14. Cp. Cassius' mention of Aeneas (I.ii.111–114).
15. Paul A. Cantor, *Shakespeare's Rome* (Ithaca: Cornell University Press, 1976), 129f.

was "the noblest man / That ever lived in the tide of times" (III.i.256–257). Antony's heart is ruled, as Cassius correctly fears, by "the ingrafted love he bears to Caesar" (II.i.184), a love which Caesar's murder turns into the most savage desire for revenge. It is not hard to see that what Antony gives to Cleopatra, or gives up for her, is meant to measure his love.[16] Not only his giving her "realms and islands" so bounteously that they are like small change "dropp'd from his pocket" (V.ii.92), but also, and even more importantly, the battles he loses or, more exactly, the losses he actively pursues, the "Kingdoms and provinces" he "kiss[es] away" (III.x.7–8), and most of all his self-inflicted death—all this is meant to measure his overflowing love.[17] The same is true of his ferocious vengeance for Caesar's assassination. However cruel and even inhuman, the vengeance is, above all, an act of giving, not of taking. Its indiscriminate savagery is intended to prove "That I did love thee, Caesar, O, 'tis true!" (III.i.194) It shows that he will spare nothing—that he will even sink to the level of a beast and scourge all human or humane feeling from the innocent as well as the guilty (III.i.254–275)—for his love. As different as they appear, Antony's terrible vengeance for Caesar is of a piece with his lavish gifts and enormous sacrifices for Cleopatra. It manifests a heart that will give up everything dear for his "strucken" "deer" (III.i.209). This "Herculean Roman" (*A & C*, I.iii.84) is nothing if not a thoroughly immoderate lover.

In contrast to Antony, "lean and hungry" Cassius is austere and unerotic, often petty and envious, and never playful.[18] No one in *Caesar* speaks of the shame of unmanliness as much or as vehemently as he. Yet, notwithstanding his ardent wish to be entirely spirited and always manly, Cassius is the leading republican example of the tension between manliness and womanliness. If Brutus is lately "with himself at war" (I.ii.45) because of his conflicting

---

16. *Ibid,* 148–156.
17. Antony of course insists that his love is too great to be measured: "There's beggary in the love than can be reckon'd." (I.i.15)
18. See esp. I.ii.189–207. See also note 11 above.

loves for Rome and Caesar, Cassius is always at war with himself because of the conflicting sides of his mixed but unstable nature—a womanly side drawing him towards others and a manly one pulling him back or away. Although he is unquestionably shrewder than Brutus, Cassius' temper is much more volatile and his passions far less restrained. Despite his strong self-contempt for any real or imagined trace of softness, his affection is stirred as easily by sorrow as his manly resentment is provoked by envy, and he often shows solicitous care for others, even his equals. He alone shows deep feeling at the news of Cicero's murder; and in sharp contrast to Brutus, who boasts that "No man bears sorrow better" and then feigns ignorance of his wife's death to impress other men with his Stoic endurance, he is willing to let others see how much he takes to heart the "insupportable and touching loss" of Portia. Cassius may have "in art" as much manly patience as Brutus to endure Portia's suicide "like a Roman," "But yet my nature," he realizes or perhaps confesses, "could not bear it so." (IV.iii.143–194) If he appears more concerned than Brutus with manliness, he does so, paradoxically, precisely because he lacks Brutus' manly constancy and reserve.

The man Cassius calls his "best friend" is his lieutenant Titinius (V.iii.35). Their friendship is probably the nearest example in *Caesar* of the sort the Republic claims to foster and Brutus suggests when he describes "hearts / Of brothers' temper" as sharing "all kind love, good thoughts, and reverence" (III.i.174–176). Cassius and Titinius do indeed have mutual regard and good will. Yet their friendship is not altogether unlike Brutus and Cassius'. It too demonstrates, though in a different way, that manliness separates honor-loving men. Appropriately, the scene at Philippi depicting their friendship also presents their deaths. Each kills himself, blaming himself at least in part for the other's death. Their suicides, however, are not the same. Whereas Titinius can feel great sorrow and affection for his commander without losing pride in his Romanness (V.iii.51–90), Cassius cannot wish to die for love of another without feeling shame at his own unmanliness. During the battle, Cassius, appealing expressly to Titinius' love for him, asks him to take his (Cassius') horse and ride to where he can tell whether certain troops are friend or enemy; and, moments later, learning that Titinius has been encircled by horsemen shouting for joy, he jumps to the wrong conclusion. Deciding then to kill himself, he says in disgust,

> O, coward that I am, to live so long,
> To see my best friend ta'en before my face.
> (V.iii.34–35)

The qualities surrounding Cassius' death are considered unmanly by all the major figures in the play. Rashness and a fatalistic despair, born of weariness and melancholic self-doubt, lead to his mistake, and his own imagined cowardice determines his act. Yet whatever else it is—and it certainly is many things[19]—Cassius' suicide is an act of friendship. Because his manliness is partly tempered by its opposite, he can wish to die for another man who soon returns the tribute in kind. But, importantly, Cassius tries to stifle his fond wish. Ashamed of all his unmanly qualities, he intends his suicide to repudiate the side of his nature that allows him to choose death thinking of anything but his honor. Ruled by his spirited heart, he kills himself, ultimately, more out of manly pride or shame than love or sorrow. The fundamentally Roman quality of his friendship with Titinius is indicated both by his suppression of his own affection and by the way each man emulates the other's brave death. But it is pointed up most of all by the more basic fact that Cassius' "best friend," though a nobleman, is not his equal. Whatever closeness there may be between them depends decisively on the distance their unmistakable inequality preserves.

As Cassius' suicide points to the limits of closeness among Roman men, so Portia's shows the limits of sharing within a Roman marriage. It marks the unattainability of the intimacy she desires from

---

19. Cassius' last words (V.iii.45–46), like Brutus' (V.v.50–51), acknowledge Caesar's personal victory, in the former case as a matter of revenge, in the latter as a matter of love.

a virtuous marriage. Portia's attempt to persuade Brutus to confide in her contains the play's only expression of intimate, erotic love. Calling herself "your self, your half," she tries to "charm" him

> . . . by my once commended beauty,
> By all your vows of love, and that great vow
> Which did incorporate and make us one.
> (II.i.271–274)

Love's desire or goal seems to inspire love's own special language. Lovers speak as if nothing at all separated them. Love not only makes or shows them equals, but even incorporates them and makes them indistinguishable parts of "one." Yet Portia makes this plea upon her knees. She says she would not have to kneel if Brutus were gentle. His customary gentleness, she suggests, implies or presupposes mutual respect. We see for ourselves, however, that Brutus is in fact much gentler with unequals than equals, and gentlest of all with his servant boy, Lucius. Portia nevertheless associates his recent ungentleness with his reticence and distance. "Within the bond of marriage," she continues, "tell me, Brutus,"

> Is it excepted I should know no secrets
> That appertain to you? Am I your self
> But, as it were, in sort or limitation,
> To keep with you at meals, comfort your bed,
> And talk to you sometimes? Dwell I but in
>   the suburbs
> Of your good pleasure? If it be no more,
> Portia is Brutus' harlot, not his wife.
> (280–287)

But because she is "his wife," Portia is indeed Brutus' "self / But, as it were, in sort or limitation." And her metaphor of "suburbs" as well as her subsequent self-inflicted wound tells us why. "You are my true and honourable wife," Brutus assures her,

> As dear to me as are the ruddy drops
> That visit my sad heart.
> (288–290)

Portia may be "dear" to him,[20] but Brutus' manly virtue rests precisely on his valuing his heart more than his blood, his public life more than his marriage. As her own metaphor of "suburbs" ironically anticipates, Portia only "visits" Brutus' heart; she does not "dwell" there. The love of fame and honor does.

Portia wishes her conjugal plea would succeed, that Brutus would tell her what "by the right and virtue of my place / I ought to know of." (269–270) Yet, as her having already taken steps to prove herself "stronger than [her] sex" (296) indicates, she never really expected it would. Recognizing that Brutus could never consider a woman his equal, she thinks she must prove herself a man to win his confidence. She realizes that, to the extent she is a woman, Brutus will never give her his trust. She fails to realize, however, that, to the extent she proves herself a man, he can no more unfold himself to her than to any other man (cp. I.ii.38–40). Since honor requires him to hide his weakness from everyone he respects and whose respect he seeks, her manly proof can succeed no better than her conjugal plea. Although Brutus at last promises to reveal his secrets, he in fact leaves home just moments later and does not return before Caesar's assassination.[21] Portia's self-inflicted wound succeeds only in shaming him to bear his troubles with greater manly patience. It inspires his prayer to be worthy of such a "noble wife" (302–303).[22]

---

20. Note that Brutus never actually says he loves Portia, though he speaks often of love.

21. Brutus cannot have returned home after II.i. When he leaves with Ligarius, he says he will reveal his plans "to thee, as we are going / To whom it must be done" (II.i.330–331); and soon afterwards they arrive together at Caesar's house to escort him to the Capitol (II.ii.108ff.). Yet there is no inconsistency in Portia's knowing in II.iv what she asks to be told in II.i. She knows as much when she asks Brutus' secret as she does later when she almost blurts it out. Whether or not she has overheard the conspirators (who leave almost immediately before she enters), it is clear from what she says and does in the earlier scene that she knows that what troubles Brutus is political and involves him in dangerous clandestine nighttime meetings. It would not require much for her to imagine the rest. Shakespeare's point, I think, is not that Portia wants to know Brutus' secret; rather, she wants him to "Tell me your counsels" (II.i.298) on the grounds that she is worthy of his trust.

22. For a contrary view of Portia and Brutus, see Mungo MacCallum, *Shakespeare's Roman Plays and Their Background* (London: Macmillan and Co., 1967), 235f., 272f., and Allan Bloom, *Shakespeare's Politics,* (New York: Basic Books, 1964), 101–103. See also Jay L. Halio, "*Harmartia,* Brutus, and the Failure of Personal Confrontation," *The Personalist,* Vol. 48, No. 1 (Winter 1967), 51–52.

Portia does not really understand the virtue she tries to emulate. She has too exalted a view of manliness to see its limitations. She recognizes that manliness involves the sort of strength that makes one superior to bodily pains and pleasures, but not that at the same time and for the same reason it also tends to make one superior to personal affection and sorrow. She is drawn to Brutus because of his virtue and imagines he would be drawn to her because of the same. Believing manliness the highest virtue, she also believes it supports or gives rise to every excellent human quality as well. She does not, or perhaps cannot, see that the virtue she most admires resists the sharing she desires as it strives for noble distinction, that it distances men from one another as it distances them from their own bodies. In both a literal and a figurative sense, the distance between Portia and Brutus leads to her death. Her suicide, which closely parallels her sudden loss of constancy when Brutus leaves home after her manly proof, is the piteous culmination of the madness caused by her extreme "impatience" for his return from the war and her desperate "grief" over the growing power of his Caesarian foes (IV.iii.151–155). Her touching death shows just how much her happiness and even her life depend on the closeness and well-being of the man she loves. Portia is the only character in *Caesar* to die solely for the love of another. Despite her real shame at the weakness of a woman's heart, hers is the only suicide not meant to prove manly strength.

No suicide is less like Portia's than Brutus'. Everyone understands his, quite properly, to have been a manly, death-defying act.[23] By killing himself in high Roman fashion, Brutus deprives his enemies of the honor of killing or capturing him. In another sense as well, however, "no man else hath honor by his death" (V.v.57). Brutus, like Caesar, dies tasting his unshared glory. The very last time he mentions Cassius is when he comes upon his and Titinius' corpses:

---

23. V.v.52ff.; cf. V.i.98–113, V.iv.*passim,* V.v.23–25. By contrast, only Titinius calls the dead Cassius "brave" (V.iii.80); despite everything, his death is seen by others as womanish (see V.iii.58ff.). It is perhaps not surprising that no one mentions Cassius in the last two scenes of the play.

> Are yet two Romans living such as these?
> The last of all the Romans, fare thee well!
> It is impossible that ever Rome
> Should breed thy fellow. Friends, I owe more tears
> To this dead man than you shall see me pay.
> I shall find time, Cassius, I shall find time.
> (V.iii.98–103)

Acknowledging the republican cause has been lost, Brutus praises Cassius in a way befitting what the Republic had always stood for. He praises him and Titinius in the same breath. He praises them, in other words, as equals, as fellow citizens, as sons of Rome (cp. V.iii.63). For himself, however, Brutus seeks preeminent distinction, not republican equality. Just as he never again mentions Portia (even in soliloquy) after stoically bidding her farewell at Sardis (IV.iii.189–191), so he forgets Cassius entirely when, about to kill himself, he envisions the glory he shall win for his life:

> Countrymen,
> My heart doth joy that yet in all my life
> I found no man but he was true to me.
> I shall have glory by this losing day
> More than Octavius and Mark Antony
> By this vile conquest shall attain unto.
> So fare you well at once; for Brutus' tongue
> Hath almost ended his life's history.
> Night hangs upon mine eyes; my bones would rest,
> That have but labour'd to attain this hour.
> (V.v.33–42)

Brutus' thoughts center on himself. He imagines his fame and glory as his alone, neither blurred nor obscured by any fellow Roman. More importantly and surprisingly, however, he sees his personal victory undiminished and perhaps even enhanced by his country's collapse. His "life's history" somehow stands above or apart from Rome. Brutus had of course claimed to be guided only by his country's good. "I know no personal cause to spurn at him," he had said of Caesar, "But for the general." (II.i.11–12) Indeed, Caesar's slaying, he had argued, was a personal sacrifice: "Not that I loved Caesar less, but that I loved Rome more."

(III.ii.22–23) Moreover, as the sacrifice of a dear friend was proof
of his fully public-spirited virtue, so too was his declared willingness to kill himself if necessary for the good of Rome: "as I slew
my best lover for the good of Rome," he had pledged at Caesar's
funeral, "I have the same dagger for myself, when it shall please
my country to need my death." (III.ii.46–48)[24] Yet, when Brutus
does finally turn his sword upon himself, Rome's welfare is absent
from his thoughts. He speaks proudly of his personal "joy" and
"glory", but while in effect eulogizing himself, he says not a word
in praise of the Republic or to lament its passing.[25] Indeed, his only
allusion to Rome is that he shall have more glory than her con-
querors.[26] His personal triumph eclipses the "vile conquest" of
Rome herself.[27]

Brutus sees his end as epitomizing and completing his virtuous
life. He regards his death as far more than a last-ditch effort to
salvage some honor from defeat, even while he understands suicide as the only honorable choice left to him (V.v.23–25; see also
V.i.98–113). His end is his crowning conquest in manly love. Just
as Lucilius bravely risks his own disgrace and death for the sake of
defending Brutus' manly honor (V.iv.12–25; see also V.v.58–59),
so, likewise, the refusal of Brutus' "poor remains of friends" to kill
him when he asks them to fills his heart with joy because he
understands their reluctance to spring from love (V.v.1–42).[28] Brutus believes the personal loyalty and sacrifices of his loving admir-
ers and friends serve to show how, to the last, he is held in esteem
by Rome. In more than the most obvious way, his death is Caesar's fitting revenge. For in Brutus' own eyes the ultimate measure
of his fame and glory is not his public-spirited devotion to his

---

24. See also I.ii.81–88.
25. Compare Brutus' silence here with what he says in the corresponding speech in
Plutarch (*Brutus*, 52.2–3): "It rejoiceth my heart," he begins, "that not one of my friends
hath failed me at my need, and I do not complain of my fortune, but only for my country's
sake. . . ." *Shakespeare's Plutarch*, ed. W. W. Skeat (London: Macmillan and Co., 1875),
151.
26. The last time Brutus mentions Rome is also the last time he mentions Cassius.
27. See ch. 3 below.
28. MacCallum, *Shakespeare's Roman Plays*, 271.

country but his countrymen's personal devotion to him.[29] In the end, the virtue of the "Soul of Rome" (II.i.321) shows itself as manliness, not patriotism. The Roman love of distinction, spurring him to master other men's hearts, separates Brutus finally not only from his friends and family, but even, or perhaps especially, from Rome herself.

Brutus does of course win singular praise and glory. Antony, who calls him "the noblest Roman of them all," says,

> His life was gentle, and all the elements
> So mix'd in him, that Nature might stand up
> And say to all the world, "This was a man!"
> (V.v.69, 73–75)

In spite of Antony's generous praise, or rather precisely because of the ambiguity of "a man," the untempered affirmation of manliness seems ultimately to issue in the repudiation of one's "mix'd" encourages the desire to have all of the manly and none of the womanly qualities. Stressing hardness, distance and assertiveness, it teaches men a willingness to risk simple cruelty and callousness in order to avoid all signs of softness, dependence and weakness. Brutus, we saw, describes "hearts / Of brothers' temper" as sharing "all kind love, good thoughts, and reverence." But his own actions, particularly in the quarrel with his "brother" Cassius, remind us that while Rome was founded by a pair of brothers, even her own traditional accounts depict her sacred origins as lying not in fraternity but fratricide.[30] Moreover, just as Shake-

---

29. This spirit of personalism allows Octavius to take into service those whom he says "serv'd Brutus" (V.v.60)—he does not say, "serv'd Rome under Brutus"—and who are recommended to him on the basis of their personal devotion. Note that even Massala speaks of Brutus as "my master" (V.v.52, 64–67).

30. It is striking and revealing that all eight of Brutus' and Cassius' references to each other as "brother" occur in the scene at Sardis and in the context of a contest of wills. The first occurs literally in the opening words of their quarrel; the second when Brutus, answering Cassius' angry charge, demands to know how he should wrong "a brother" if he does not wrong even his enemies (IV.iii.37–39). The third reference occurs when Cassius, "aweary of the world," despairingly shames himself by acknowledging he is "Hated by one he loves; brav'd by his brother" (IV.iii.95); and the fourth not long after the quarrel itself when Cassius, commanding "Hear me, good brother." (211), tries (but fails) to counter Brutus' willful overruling of his more prudent battle plans and then is forced for the first time to

speare frequently reminds us of the literal meaning of Brutus' name,[31] so he also reminds us that those same Roman accounts say Romulus was nurtured by a she-wolf.[32] Shakespeare, I think, truly admires Roman virtue. In *Caesar* he shows that such excellence does indeed involve more than human strength. But Shakespeare's appreciation of manly virtue is by no means unqualified. His portrayal of Rome, like Rome's own traditional accounts of her foundations, suggests that the Romans ultimately debase the human in order to elevate the man.

---

defer explicitly to his will (223–224). The next two references seem, by contrast, to stress reconciliation and even amity. Just a moment or so later, Cassius, taking leave, begs his "dear brother" not to let "such division" ever come " 'tween our souls" again; and Brutus, assuring him that everything is well, bids "Good night, good brother." (232–236) Despite one's first impression, however, Brutus' use of "good brother" does not reflect a restored equality or mutual respect between him and Cassius. Coming in the general wake of their quarrel and less than a dozen lines after Cassius explicitly submits to his will, his use of the phrase springs from the generosity of a conqueror, not the manly esteem of an equal. Brutus can afford to show Cassius greater friendliness and even praise him more highly than ever before (231) precisely because Cassius, having been forced to acknowledge the inequality in their friendship, can no longer threaten his domination. Indeed, Brutus' valediction "Good night, good brother." comes in direct response to Cassius' valediction "Good night, my lord." (236) At no other time does Cassius ever call anyone his "lord." In accordance with all this, the last two references to "brother" both involve Brutus' issuing Cassius military orders (247,303). The only other time either man is spoken of as the other's "brother" (II.i.7) directly precedes the meeting of conspirators when Brutus, forcing Cassius to bow to his moral domination, supplants him as the conspiracy's leader.

31. Most esp. at III.i.77.

32. I.ii.1–11; for the connection between the Lupercal race and the story of Romulus, see Plutarch, *Romulus* 21.3–8, and Ovid, *Fasti* II.381ff.

Two

Caesarism and the End of Republican Rome: Act I, scene i

SHOULD CAESAR BE KILLED TO SAVE THE ROMAN REPUBLIC AND THE political life it supports? Caesar's assassins show by their words and deed that they consider Rome's degraded and degrading condition reversible. Brutus makes their underlying premise clear when, defending the assassination, he asks the people rhetorically, "Had you rather Caesar were living, and die all slaves, than that Caesar were dead, to live all free men?" (III.ii.23–25) As Caesar's living would doom Rome to lasting slavery, so his death, Brutus believes, promises continued freedom. The Republic, however, scarcely outlives Caesar. Within hours of the assassination, "Brutus and Cassius /Are rid like madmen through the gates of Rome" (III.ii.270–271) and never return. Explanations of this outcome have generally focused on the personal shortcomings of the leading conspirators, particularly Brutus, suggesting that with better leadership their cause might have prevailed.[1] The republican leaders' personal char-

---

1. The best of these critics is Allan Bloom. Although sometimes equivocating (e.g., "The only way to suppress Caesar would be to establish another tyranny."), Bloom emphasizes that "the failure of the [conspirators'] plot can be traced directly to the victory of Brutus's

21

acteristics are no doubt very important to their defeat. Yet *Caesar* begins in such a way as to indicate the even greater importance of the political regime. While none of the principal characters appears until I.ii,[2] the opening scene depicts the condition of Rome's republican regime. This essay, concentrating on that much-neglected scene,[3] examines Shakespeare's presentation of the late Republic. I.i, in many respects a puzzling frontispiece to the drama it introduces,[4] suggests that the outcome of events in *Caesar* is essentially an outgrowth of the regime, that owing to the fact that, politically, the form is most formative, Caesar's death is necessarily the end, not the salvation, of republican Rome.

The Liberation of the Personal or the Private

Caesar begins amid civil disorder. As I.i opens, the tribune Flavius is reprimanding a group of recalcitrant plebians, ordering them home. Our first glimpse of Caesar's Rome shows the tribunes, whose ancient office had been established to protect the people

---

principles over Cassius' prudence" and that, to succeed, "The plot should have been led by one man who had the qualities of both Brutus and Cassius." (*Shakespeare's Politics* [New York: Basic Books, 1964], 82, 96, 92) See also his "Political Philosophy and Politics," *American Political Science Review*, 54 (June 1960), 463: "[O]nly a man who combined the virtues of Brutus and Cassius could have successfully opposed Caesar and re-established the Roman republic." Bloom's interpretation stresses the corruption of both the Republic's enemies within the noble class and the people, but ignores the corruption, as distinguished from the personal shortcomings, of the Republic's principal defenders.

See also John Palmer, *Political Characters of Shakespeare* (London: Macmillan and Co., 1961), 1–64; Matthew N. Proser, *The Heroic Image in Five Shakespearean Tragedies* (Princeton University Press, 1965), 10–50; Kenneth Muir, *Shakespeare's Tragic Sequence* (London: Hutchinson University Library, 1972), 42–54; Ernest Schanzer, *The Problem Plays of Shakespeare* (New York: Schocken Books, 1965), esp. 35f. and 67f.

2. Not only does none appear in I.i, but when first presented all appear together at the start of I.ii.

3. Although critics generally agree that I.i of *Caesar,* like other first scenes in Shakespeare, introduces the play's "underlying forces" (John Dover Wilson, The New Shakespeare *Julius Caesar* [London: Cambridge University Press, 1947], 101), their observations on the scene have been little more than summary or cursory. Perhaps the most extensive treatment is by Brents Stirling, *The Populace in Shakespeare* (New York: Columbia University Press, 1947), 25ff. and 48f.

4. Why is the introduction largely a semi-comic dialogue when the rest of the play, in keeping with its "sober, streamlined" tone, seems to have an "absence of all comic matter"? And why is a central part of its frontispiece a quibbling cobbler's dialogue when "a sparing use of metaphor and word-play, coupled with a remarkable economy and directness of speech by all the characters, secures the 'dignified and unadorned simplicity—a Roman simplicity, perhaps', which, as Bradley says, and Sir Edmund Chambers agrees, is the distinguishing feature of the play"? (Wilson, *Caesar,* xi–xii)

against the nobility's arrogance, now apparently forced to defend the Republic against the people themselves.

Civil commotion stemming from popular unrest is, however, endemic to Rome's mixed regime. *Coriolanus,* set at the dawn of the Republic and depicting the establishment of the tribunate, also begins amid popular dissension in the streets.[5] But the people in that play are altogether different from those in *Caesar.* They are needy, hard-working, insecure, grateful, and relatively self-restrained, while their late-republican counterparts are none of these. Although it is apparently "a labouring day" (4), not a "holiday" (2), the workers in *Caesar* are "idle" (1). They are not in their shops or even dressed for work. Instead of displaying the tools and other outward signs of his trade, the carpenter is wearing his best clothes (8, 48). He lacks his "rule" (7) in more than one sense. According to the angry Flavius, he and the other artisans belong at "home" (1) in their shops. No doubt the people's unruliness shows that they have forgotten their place, but Flavius goes considerably further than one might expect. Besides ignoring that it is indeed a holiday, the ancient feast of Lupercal (67),[6] the tribune's attempt to restore the traditional authority of his office involves a major distortion. His traditionalism amounts to revisionism, for he plainly suggests that the people not only deserve no political part in Rome, but in fact never had one. Judging from his reprimand, one would suppose they were never "Dissentious numbers pest'ring [the] streets" (*Cor.* IV.vi.7), but were always decorous, even to the point of being apolitical. Frightened by Caesar's growing absorption of his traditional powers (68–75), Flavius nearly forgets his purpose. In trying to save his office, he seems willing, even eager, to disen-

---

5. Indicating well the character of the Roman Republic and its mixed regime, Shakespeare's Roman plays—or, more accurately, *Coriolanus* and *Caesar* but not the post-republican *Antony and Cleopatra*—began with scenes of popular unrest and, as Bloom points out (*Shakespeare's Politics,* 106, n. 4), "are the only [Shakespearean plays] in which the people as a whole is an actor." For the connection between political turmoil and political freedom in Rome, see Machiavelli, *Discourses,* I.3–10.

6. This important fact is at once underscored and obscured by Shakespeare's presenting Caesar's triumph and the Lupercal as occurring on a single day. Historically they were four months apart. For the fact that the Lupercal was not a workday, see Macrobius, *Saturnalia,* I.16.6.

franchise those who have elected him to it. He seems to confuse the people's former submission to the tribunes with their never having had any political power at all.[7] Rome, one would think, never had a mixed regime.

Yet, for all his unruliness, the carpenter is almost docile compared with the group's ringleader, the cobbler. Whereas the carpenter answers Flavius directly and even respectfully, the cobbler displays nothing but insolent levity and mock respect as he answers the tribunes' questions with glib puns, vexing evasions, and even threats which taunt both them and their concerns. What they take most seriously and even their seriousness he finds fit for trifling.

When first asked "what trade are you?" he replies, "Truly, sir, in respect of a fine workman, I am but, as you would say, a cobbler." (10–11) "Cobbler" can mean either a shoemaker or a bungler. That the tribunes have to ask thrice more before either thinks of the former and more obvious meaning is less surprising than may appear, for the cobbler deliberately frames his answers to suggest the latter. Ironically, if explicitly, adopting their low view of him, he responds to their main, though tacit, concern. And taking his cue from Marullus' own unwitting pun on "rule," he formulates a series of answers than can refer equally to his particular trade or to his worrisome role as a citizen. And even though they persist in asking only about the one, the tribunes really care only about the other. Their concerns are entirely political. It is thus not so much a matter of their own bungling, but rather a sign of their preoccupation, that the tribunes are slow to grasp the answer they are demanding and hear instead only the oblique political implications of the cobbler's quibbles. Absorbed by the political, they are deaf to the most obvious meaning of his words.

The cobbler knows exactly how to vex the tribunes. His impudence centers on distinguishing thrice in his peculiar way between what he is or does "truly" (10, 21, 29) and what he is or does

---

7. For the tribunes' manipulation of the people, see *Coriolanus*, II.i.192–257, II.iii.129–253, III.iii.1–29 and Paul A. Cantor, *Shakespeare's Rome* (Ithaca: Cornell Univ. Press, 1976), 88f.

"indeed" (14, 23, 30). All his prevarications stem from his dual roles as shoemaker and citizen. His longest and most obscure answer (21–26), which combines proverbs and puns, equally denies and affirms that his concerns are simply private and that his practices are uncorrupt: he does and does not meddle in politics. Whereas the first (10–19) of his three sets of answers, insinuating that he himself or his "conscience" is his own authority, threatens to punish the tribunes if they are angry with him, the second (21–26) suggests that for a price his handiwork can provide "proper men" with a safe footing. As his final answer bears out, he is interested in what profits or gratifies himself in merely private ways and is indifferent to the effect of his private concerns on the public life of Rome. Asked why he is not in his shop and why he leads the others about the streets, he explains:

> Truly, sir, to wear out their shoes, to get myself into more work. But indeed, sir, we make holiday to see Caesar, and to rejoice in his triumph. (29–31)

While the cobbler's "deeds" are political in their effect, his "true" motive is private gain and enjoyment. He is interested in public things only insofar as they are not truly public. His relation to Caesar (who is mentioned here for the first time) is thus radically new in that no public concern links them. The city as such is no part of their relation.[8] The only link the cobbler recognizes, and indeed the only one that exists, is not the city of Rome or the public office Caesar occupies (which is never mentioned in the play),[9] but purely private concerns. Caesar's rule is entirely personal. Caesar offers the cobbler "bread and circuses,"[10] and that is enough for him.

---

8. The word "city" never occurs in *Caesar*. By contrast, as Michael Platt mentions (*Rome and Romans According to Shakespeare* [Salzburg Studies in English Literature: Institut für Englische Sprache und Literatur, 1976], 57, n.3), it occurs in *Coriolanus* more often (39 times) than in any other Shakespearean play. Similarly, the speech-headings in *Caesar* never refer to the people as "citizens"; in *Coriolanus* they always do.
9. By the same token, Brutus' is (I.iii.142–144).
10. Platt, *Rome and Romans*, 176.

The Ascendancy of Personal Loyalty

The second tribune, Marullus, is much more provoked by the people's forgetting Pompey and rejoicing in Caesar's triumph than by their pursuit of private interests. He indignantly reminds them that Caesar's triumph marks the defeat of their fellow Roman and former benefactor, Pompey. Far from deserving rejoicing, Caesar's victory requires a defense. Civil war, it seems, is altogether different from foreign war. Unlike victory over a foreign enemy, Caesar's victory over a fellow Roman citizen needs, as Plutarch says, his excuse "unto the gods and men that he was compelled to do [what] he did."[11] And since only necessity can excuse the deed, nothing can excuse its celebration. Marullus therefore connects a charge of impiety to his rebuke. He says the people's celebration shows the sort of ingratitude the gods punish most severely. Only humble prayers can spare Rome from the god-sent "plague / That needs must light on this ingratitude." (54–55)

If Marullus is right, the gods take an active interest in Roman affairs. Gratitude must have a superhuman support. But it is unclear whether he means that the people have been ungrateful only towards Pompey or towards the gods as well. Could Rome's gods care enough about Pompey to punish Rome indiscriminately for the celebration of his sons' defeat? Whatever the case, Marullus finds nothing impious in Rome's foreign conquests. Agreeing with Flavius, who is unconcerned with the gods (55–60; cp. 66–69), he fully endorses Rome's vast expansion through war (32–55). Impiety, it seems, attaches to the unbounded ambitions of men, not of cities.

Marullus' harangue appears at first to be grounded squarely in traditional republican principles: the unlimited greatness of Rome is one thing; that of any individual Roman, quite another. But on closer examination there is nothing republican about his speech. Marullus thrice speaks of Rome (33, 36, 42) but uses the name only in its loose sense, never as a distinctive regime or way of life.[12]

---

11. *Caesar* 56.4; *Shakespeare's Plutarch*, ed. W. W. Skeat (London: Macmillan and Co., 1875), 91.
12. See *Coriolanus* III.i.238–240.

It denotes a place or collection of things along the Tiber. "Rome" is strictly speaking subpolitical, referring to the materials, not to the political form, of the city. Moreover, Marullus' rebuke is not just nonrepublican but in fact antirepublican. What he says is more compatible with monarchy than with republicanism inasmuch as his indignant reminder of Pompey contradicts traditional republican equality and the ingratitude he accuses the people of is ingratitude not towards Rome or the Republic but towards a particular Roman or Roman family. The people are "cruel men of Rome" (36), "worse than senseless things" (35), not for willingly abandoning the Republic, but for hard-heartedly forgetting "great Pompey" (42) and celebrating the defeat of "Pompey's blood" (51). Thus, even as he summons a demonstration of piety, Marullus is silent about the obligations the people, as citizens, owe Rome. The piety he calls for has nothing to do with traditional republican virtue or civic piety. Marullus takes for granted that the household, not the city, is the center of the people's lives and addresses them as private persons or, more exactly, as fathers. The people are to pray for divine forgiveness for rejoicing in the defeat of the sons of a father whose own triumph they, as fathers (40), often celebrated. Moreover, they are to offer their prayers in the privacy of their own houses (53–55).

The issue was essentially the same, but the tenor entirely different, when Menenius spoke of how the Roman gods forbade the people's execution of Coriolanus:

> Now the good gods forbid
> That our renowned Rome, whose gratitude
> Toward her deserved children is enroll'd
> In Jove's own book, like an unnatural dam
> Should now eat up her own!
> (III.i.289–293)

The gods Menenius invoked were the gods of Rome, gods of the city. They sustained the Republic by upholding the belief that there is nothing higher than Rome or beyond the city. Essentially civic or public, they linked individuals together by linking them first and foremost to the city. Rome, which the gods defended as a community, was (or was piously thought to be) the Romans' common source and end.[13] The Romans were Rome's citizens because they were first of all her "children."[14] The gods Marullus invokes, on the other hand, have no public aspect. Rather than elevate the public over the private, they sanctify the private.[15] They defend the family, not the city. The city is no part of their worship, but is completely absent from the obligations they enforce among men.

Marullus ultimately urges personal loyalty, not patriotism, above all else. As he presents it, Caesar's triumph is unworthy of the people's rejoicing, not because he is Rome's enemy (or even the people's), but because he is Pompey's and Pompey was their hero. His indignation is stirred, not because they have made themselves slaves to some great hero, but merely because they are fickle in their love. In a most important sense, the real issue between him and the people is not republicanism versus Caesarism but rather which great hero should be Rome's Caesar.[16]

The Resolution of "Ancient Malice"

Marullus' declamation demonstrates the evil it inveighs against. To a large and probably even decisive extent, however, both he and Flavius are forced by the revolutionary situation they deplore to attack Caesar on Caesarian grounds. Like Marullus' speech, Flavius' opening reprimand of the idle workers is fundamentally at variance with republicanism. For one may argue, as indeed the cobbler's answers suggest, that the concerns of artisans qua artisans are indifferent to political freedom. Inasmuch as they are essentially private, they are better served under a monarch than by the

---

13. Bloom, *Shakespeare's Politics*, 78.

14. See *Caesar*, I.ii.171 and V.iii.63.

15. In Marullus' description of Pompey's triumphs, private buildings literally tower over Rome's "walls and battlements" (37–39). For Pompey's antitraditional triumphs, see Plutarch, *Pompey*, 14, 43–45.

16. Bloom (*Shakespeare's Politics*, 82) mistakes the tribunes' significance when he says they are "defending the traditional role of the senatorial class, so that the constitution can remain intact." Although they are "courageous opponents of Caesar," the tribunes do not defend the traditional regime.

public-spirited life of the Republic.[17] Flavius nevertheless encourages these concerns. Instead of attempting to revive some public or class interest among the people, he urges them to return to their private pursuits. Their "home" is not the city but their private shops within it. Flavius' aim, it seems, is not to recoup the people's traditional support and use it against Caesar, but to eliminate their political role completely. The only hope of stopping Caesar, he seems to think, is to drive the people out of Rome's political life.

In a certain sense, Flavius may be right. The reason he gives for fearing Caesar is virtually the same one the earlier tribunes had for fearing Coriolanus. If Coriolanus were elected consul, "Then our office may / During his power go sleep." (II.i.209–210) Flavius, however, fears a permanent demise. Referring to the ornaments that have been placed on Caesar's statues, he warns Marullus that

> These growing feathers pluck'd from Caesar's wing
> Will make him fly at an ordinary pitch,
> Who else would soar above the view of men
> And keep us all in servile fearfulness.
> (72–75)

Yet, despite his alarm, neither he nor Marullus attempts what their counterparts did so effectively to bring Coriolanus down. They attempt just two things. They try to shame the people for betraying Pompey and have some success (61–62); and they proceed to "Disrobe the images" (64), for which they are themselves quickly stripped of power (I.ii.282–283). Most importantly, they do nothing to arouse the people's "ancient malice" (*Cor.* II.i.215) towards their traditional enemies and especially towards Rome's great military heroes.

---

17. A comparison of *Coriolanus* and *Caesar* suggests a connection between the decline of republican virtue and a rise in the arts. Whereas the people's specific trades are emphasized right at the start of *Caesar,* they are never specified in *Coriolanus.* In the earlier and poorer Republic, the people are citizen-soldiers first and tradesmen second. See n. 8 above. In addition, in *Caesar* we find both foreigners and poets, neither of which appear in *Coriolanus.* Most importantly, in *Caesar* even the republican leaders—indeed, especially Brutus, Cassius and Cicero—are shown to be inclined towards the cosmopolitan doctrines of Greek teachers and hence away from the ancient gods and traditions of Rome. See, further, Plutarch, *Marcellus,* 21, *Pyrrhus,* 10, and *Cato the Elder,* 22–23.

They attempt nothing of the sort because they know there is nothing to be done. The fundamental realignment of domestic factions that constitutes Caesarism precludes a revival of the class antagonisms underlying the old regime. The basis of the old regime was a generally, if not perfectly, rigid class division between the people and the nobles. As we see in *Coriolanus*,[18] the Republic rested on a delicate balance of power between its two hostile classes. Its preservation required that the two hostile factions recognize their mutual need and yet never overcome their mutual antagonism, and that neither party use its weight to support a particular person—whether a Marius or a Sulla, a Pompey or a Caesar—in its struggle to remain free from the other's domination. Thus, while the people had to trust only the tribunes to protect their interests, the nobles had to remain steadfast in their determination to manage Roman affairs and refrain as a matter of pride from turning to the people to help arbitrate their disputes or further their personal ambitions. Coriolanus, although an inveterate enemy of Rome's mixed regime, epitomizes the necessary conditions for its survival.

By Caesar's time, however, these conditions had virtually disappeared. Class solidarity had cracked, and radically new alliances emerged. Members of the nobility had deserted their own rank and taken the people's side, at once splitting the Senate into hostile factions and weakening the tribunes whose old cause the new popular leaders now espoused. Instead of the two offices being counterpoised, each curbing the other's power and ambitions, the consulate increasingly became a kind of tribunate, only with the enormous wealth and prestige of foreign conquests now at its disposal. And so, as we see in I.i, the "ancient malice" the people used to have particularly towards patricians like Coriolanus has been replaced by their "saucy" (18) behavior towards their traditional protectors. The tribunes' cause is no longer theirs. The people's

---

18. For an excellent discussion of Shakespeare's presentation of the political workings of the early Republic, see Cantor, *Shakespeare's Rome*, 55–71.

cause has shifted from the defense of democratic elements within a mixed regime to the establishment of a monarchical regime claiming to rule in the name of the people. It is no surprise that the tribunes suppress the fact that Pompey's defeat in the recent civil war was also the Senate's defeat. They have every reason to ignore the important connection between Pompey and the hated Senate. What is singularly remarkable, however, is that even though "the common people at Rome never longed for [any]thing more than they did to see the office of tribune set up again" after Sulla had pulled it down,[19] the tribunes never suggest that the people owe Pòmpey their gratitude for having restored it. Just as they manage to avoid mentioning Caesar by name in front of the people,[20] so too, and for the same reason, they never mention their own office in front of them. In a way they are as "tongue-tied" (62) as the momentarily intimidated people. Roman politics has so thoroughly lost its public character that the tribunes have no republican ground left from which to attack Caesar or defend his enemies. "[T]he spirit of Caesar" (II.i.167)—the spirit of personalism —[21] has already overthrown the Republic's mixed regime.

The Neglect of Republican Tradition

The people have forgotten more than just Pompey, however. As noted earlier, none remembers the feast of Lupercal. The new holiday they make for Caesar overshadows an ancient holiday tracing back to Rome's sacred foundations.[22] Caesar's triumph has caused the people to neglect Rome's ancestral past.

---

19. Plutarch, *Pompey,* 21.5; trans. Sir Thomas North (London: The Tudor Translations, 1896), IV.226, with modernized spelling and punctuation.

20. Note the periphrasis at ll. 50–51.

21. L. C. Knights ("Shakespeare and Political Wisdom: A Note on the Personalism of *Julius Caesar* and *Coriolanus,*" *Sewanee Review,* 61 [1953], 43–55) uses the term "personalism" to distinguish the private man and his personal life from the public figure and his political life. Knights' narrow use of the term reflects a strong antipolitical bias which can be seen in his contention that the private or the personal realm is always more real and more important than anything found in the political world.

22. See n. 6 above. For the connection between the Lupercal and Romulus, see the citation in ch. 1, n. 32 above.

This circumstance is especially important because the observance of republican order is the observance of traditional order. Roman republicanism at least tacitly identifies the old or the ancestral with the good.[23] It therefore rests on preserving the integrity and dignity of well-established ways. The pious tribune demonstrates this well. Marullus was forced to tolerate Flavius' implicit denial of the ancestral holiday in order to check the people's more pressing abuse. However, after the people depart, he balks at his colleague's plan to go towards the Capitol and "Disrobe the images" if he finds "them deck'd with ceremonies." (64–65) He evidently believes that such an act on the Lupercal would be a sacrilege (66–67). As concerned as Flavius was by the artisans' failure to display the outward signs of their trades, Marullus is even more concerned that he himself might violate a sacred obligation or prohibition. For him, the outward forms of piety do not serve simply to keep the plebeians in order. They are sacred and command reverence in their own right. They are an integral part of Roman life.

Since the Romans have always clung to the old order chiefly out of reverence for the ancestral, such things as names, titles, rites, and ceremonies possess the utmost significance in the Republic. They define the regime by establishing or manifesting its public order. In

---

23. See I.ii.6–9, 111–114, 148–159; I.iii.80–84; and II.i.52–54. See also I.iii.171, II.i.136–140, and V.iv.2–6.

We might also note that Brutus and Cassius' ambivalent references to their ancestors point up the central problem of the Republic. Cassius insists that Rome's "ancestors" were republican (I.iii.80–84) and yet reveres Aeneas as "our great ancestor" (I.ii.111). Brutus speaks of no ancestors prior to his famous namesake, but his strongest reference presents a confusion similar to Cassius': "Shall Rome stand under one man's awe? What, Rome? / My ancestors did from the streets of Rome / The Tarquin drive, when he was call'd a king." (II.i.52–54) Brutus speaks as if his ancestors had restored rather than founded the Republic. Cassius, however, goes even further. In the same speech in which he reminds Brutus of the need to live up to his ancestor's name, he implicitly dates the Republic from the time of "the great flood" (I.ii.133–159). Rome, in other words, has no prerepublican past whatsoever. The republican formula honoring tradition presupposes something like a Golden Age. All progress is a return to perfect (republican) beginnings. What this means is indicated by Caesar, who never speaks of his ancestors but declares instead, "Danger knows full well / That Caesar is more dangerous than he. / We are two lions litter'd in one day, / And I the elder and more terrible." (II.ii.44–47) The traditional formula honoring tradition honors manliness, not age (cp. Cassius' estimation of Aeneas with his estimation of Aeneas' father, "old Anchises," [I.ii.111ff.]. The earliest times were the best of times because they were most dangerous and terrible and therefore most warlike and manly.

a most important sense, the Roman Republic *is* its outward forms and fixed conventions, especially in the minds of the people to whom names seem to mean everything and substance nothing,[24] and especially since Rome's mixed regime was always ruled largely in hidden or indirect ways. Owing above all to the fundamental obscurity of what really constitutes the Republic or Rome herself —an obscurity stemming to a large extent precisely from the city's endless partisan strife—Rome's traditional forms are, and always were, primarily what most Romans consider Rome to be. The symbols are somehow seen as the substance.[25]

But while Rome's republicanism rests decisively on preserving the sanctity of ancestral conventions, that same pious attachment to fixed forms finally facilitates the regime's corruption. In this (as in virtually everything else important concerning the Republic), what is in one respect a vital strength is in another respect, or becomes under different circumstances, a serious danger. Commenting on what happens at the Lupercal when Antony offers Caesar a crown, Plutarch observes that the Roman people at Caesar's time "suffered all things subjects should do by commandment of their kings, and yet could not abide the name of king, detesting it as the utter destruction of their liberty."[26] And Casca's eyewitness report (I.ii.212ff.) surely bears Plutarch out: republican forms remain, but they lack republican life.[27] The people, bound by tradition, cling to established forms; but precisely because of their traditionalism, they do so finally in such a mechanical way[28] as not to notice or perhaps care that the forms have lost their content. We see this demonstrated again, and most importantly, at Caesar's funeral

---

24. Bloom, *Shakespeare's Politics*, 90.

25. For a discussion of the importance of rites and ceremonies in *Caesar* from a different point of view, see Brents Stirling, *Unity in Shakespearean Tragedy* (New York: Columbia Univ. Press, 1956), 40–54.

26. *Antony*, 12.3–4; Skeat, *Shakespeare's Plutarch*, 164.

27. So, too, with Casca's own republicanism. Republican sentiment or spirit survives mainly on his lips and mainly in the form of stock expressions. Cp. I.ii.239–247 with *Coriolanus*, I.i.48–49, II.i.218–223, III.iii.120–123, IV.vi.95–98; see also *ibid.*, II.iii.56–57 and III.i.66.

28. Consider I.i.2–5.

when the people voice their approval of Brutus' reasons for killing Caesar by shouting their wish that he "be Caesar" (III.ii.52). The forbidden title of "king" has become one thing; "Caesar," quite another. The people's strict adherence to republican tradition has finally degenerated into a kind of literalness.[29]

Shakespeare suggests that literalism is peculiarly a late-republican form of corruption. It is at once the degradation and the fulfillment of republican principles. The people's essential conservatism, rooted in a fear of the unknown and hence attaching them chiefly to accustomed forms, supports and is supported in turn by the republican equation of the old and the good. But the people's native conservatism eventually corrupts their republicanism, for ultimately it attaches them more to tradition as such than to republican tradition. And so, as the people's traditionalism is primary while their republicanism is derivative, Rome's ancestral forms first harden and petrify before breaking up and crumbling away. As the cobbler's clever punning anticipates, the neglect of republican tradition is, more correctly, the fossilization rather than the outright obliteration of republican traditions.[30]

The End of Public Oratory and Republican Freedom

I.i is usually understood to prepare us for the mob's crucial change of sentiment at Caesar's funeral by showing the people's affections and support shifting from Pompey to Caesar.[31] Although not wrong,

---

29. "Caesar's death almost becomes a tragedy of semantics." (J. L. Simmons, *Shakespeare's Pagan World* [Charlottesville, Va.: Univ. of Virginia Press, 1973], 78.

30. Hence the peculiar mixture of traditionalism and antirepubilcanism in Caesar's first appearance. Contrary to what I.i leads us to expect, when Caesar first appears (I.ii.1–24) he ignores his own celebration and what he says seems in perfect accord with traditional piety. Not only is he particularly concerned with observing every "ceremony" of the Lupercal, but he emphasizes that his punctilious observance of the "holy chase" rests solely on the authority of Rome's ancestors. What "our elders say" alone determines what Caesar says. Just as the people seem to have forgotten the old holiday as they make a new one for Caesar, so he seems to have forgotten his own triumph as he prepares to celebrate the old holiday. Caesar's traditionalism, however, is by no means traditionally republican. Its antitraditional character can be seen precisely in his manner of bidding the traditional observance. Caesar commands like a king, and Antony responds like a most submissive subject: "When Caesar says, 'Do this,' it is perform'd." Antony's sole authority is Caesar, who, as we see in the brief scene, is treated like a king not only by his partisans, but by his enemies as well.

31. E.g., by Stirling, *Populace in Shakespeare*, 26.

this view is misleading insofar as it ignores the decisive differences between republicanism and Caesarism and particularly the connection between the rise of "the cult of personality" and the decline of republicanism in Rome.[32] To accept the usual interpretation as complete is, in other words, not to see Rome's late corruption for what it really is.[33] I.i. does of course prepare us directly for what happens at Caesar's funeral. It does this in part by what it shows about the liberation of private concerns and the consequent ascendancy of personal loyalty: the cobbler's last answer, in particular, foreshadows Antony's conclusion to his funeral oration when he elevates Caesar to "a Caesar" while at the same time announcing Caesar's private bequests to the people (III.ii.237–254). But I.i does this in part also by what the cobbler's conversation as a whole suggests about the decline in the power and importance of public speech in Rome, a decline that results from the resolution of Rome's traditional class strife and the consequent loss of republican authority. That Brutus' and Antony's funeral orations are among the most celebrated political speeches in Shakespeare, and certainly the most celebrated in the Roman plays, has tended to draw attention away from something crucial about them. They are the consummation, which is to say, the end, of political oratory in Rome.

The counterpart in *Coriolanus* of the quibbling cobbler's dialogue with the hard-pressed tribunes is Menenius' dialogue with the people and particularly the "pretty tale" (I.i.76ff.) he tells to quiet their rebellion. The Republic was always ruled by public speech and hence ultimately by authoritative opinion. Indeed,

---

32. Platt, e.g., sees no conflict between the people's hero-worship and republicanism. He argues that in forgetting Pompey the people "have forgotten themselves—or rather that part of themselves which is eager for politics." (*Rome and Romans,* 176) For an illuminating discussion of the fact that "the real danger to the Republic stems, not from plebeian disrespect for nobility, but from the readiness with which the plebeians are willing to fall down before the military heroes of the city," see Cantor, *Shakespeare's Rome,* 74f.

33. This does not seem to disturb some critics. Schanzer writes: "Political issues, such as the choice between a republican and a monarchic form of government for Rome," are "not a concern of the play itself but merely of some of the play's characters." (*Problem Plays,* 68) Similarly, Palmer, in his chapter on Brutus, writes: "Shakespeare, in his political plays, presents political situations and characters, but his supreme interest is always in the private person." (*Political Characters,* 54)

Coriolanus and *Caesar* both begin by stressing rhetoric's political importance to Rome.[34] Their opening scenes show not only that popular unrest is characteristic of republican freedom, but also the closely connected point that governing men through speech is distinctly republican.[35] But while *Coriolanus* demonstrates that public speech is at once a cause of the early Republic's civil disorder and an indispensible means to control its violence,[36] the first scene of *Caesar* indicates that much of its traditional power has faded. The cobbler, signifying the people's growing unwillingness or inability to be governed in this manner, hardly allows himself to be ruled by the tribune's speech, and his recalcitrance is matched both by what he says and how he says it. In this most important respect, the people's traditional spokesmen are first "put to silence" (I.ii.283) by the people themselves.

Political oratory goes together in Rome with republican freedom, not imperial rule.[37] It thrives on factional strife and even strives to perpetuate it since the major rewards of such speech come from kindling rather than quenching republican fires. Just as political oratory's importance diminishes where the people are well-behaved and ready to obey their rulers, so its importance increases where there is no single guiding hand.[38] The political importance of rhetoric thus reflects the political importance of the people. This relation is still evident—indeed, most evident—at Caesar's funeral where the speeches, like the rhetoric of the whole conspiracy, are directed entirely to the people.[39] Brutus' and An-

---

34. Note the opening two lines of *Coriolanus*. Note also that the predominant mode of speech in *Caesar*, often even in private conversations, is rhetorical. See Mark Van Doren, *Shakespeare* (New York: Holt, Rinehart and Winston, 1939), 180–186. For the contrasting position of poetry in Rome, consider Brutus' remark at IV.iii.123–127. III.iii suggests that an Emperor or a Caesar might welcome or even befriend poets as part of his general encouragement of private concerns. See n. 17 above.

35. The words "voice" and "voices" appear far more often in *Coriolanus* (48 times) than in any other Shakespearean play. In II.iii alone they occur 23 times.

36. See I.i.1–208, II.i.192–246, II.ii.34–157, II.iii.44–253, III.i.24–335, III.ii.25–145, and III.iii *passim*.

37. See *Caesar*, I.ii.183–186, 275–283, II.ii.60ff.; III.i.31ff.; III.ii *passim*.

38. See Tacitus, *A Dialogue on Oratory*, esp. 36.

39. III.i.79–110, 236–242; III.ii *passim*.

tony's orations are as much tributes to the people's political importance as tributes to Caesar himself.

The celebrated funeral orations are also, however, the last exam-
ples of political rhetoric in Shakespeare's Rome. In contrast to
what we see throughout *Coriolanus* and in the first three acts of
Caesar, no one in the last two acts of *Caesar* or anywhere in the
postrepublican *Antony and Cleopatra* ever thinks it necessary or
even useful to persuade the people of anything. Once they drive the
republican faction from Rome, the people cease to be an important
political force. Their power, dissolving with their traditional enemies' expulsion, ends with the last speech addressed to them or
just moments later when—in the play's most vivid and grotesque
instance of literal-mindedness or punning—the mob, aroused by
Antony's words to (as one plebeian ambiguously cries) "Pluck
down forms, windows, any thing" (III.ii.261), kills Cinna the poet
simply because his name is the same as a conspirator's (III.iii.26–34).
III.iii thus dramatically demonstrates what I.i anticipates. The people's political power ends in a grotesque climax of murderous
literalism. Just as Caesar's funeral marks the final destruction, not
the preservation, of the moribund Republic, so the cobbler's peculiar conversation bespeaks the approaching end of political oratory and hence the death of republican freedom in Rome.

Three

Politics and the Ethics of Intention: Brutus' Glorious Failure

EDWARD GIBBON, THE HISTORIAN OF ROME, BEGINS HIS STUDY OF BRUTUS by drawing attention to the wide discrepancy between his illustrious reputation for patriotic virtue and his actual contribution to his country:

> The memory of Caesar, celebrated as it is, has not been transmitted down to posterity with such uniform and encreasing applause as that of his PATRIOT ASSASSIN. Marc Antony acknowledged the rectitude of his Intentions. Augustus refused to violate his Statues. All the great Writers of the succeeding Age, enlarged on his Praises, and more than two hundred Years after the Establishment of the Imperial Government the Character of Brutus was studied as the Perfect Idea of Roman Virtue. In England as in France, in modern Italy as in ancient Rome, his name has always been mentioned with Respect by the Adherents of Monarchy, and pronounced with Enthusiasm by the Friends of Freedom. It may seem rash and invidious to appeal from the Sentence of Ages; yet surely I may be permitted to enquire, in what consisted THE DIVINE VIRTUE OF BRUTUS?
> The few Patriots, who by a bold and well concerted Enterprize, have delivered their Country from foreign or

domestic Slavery, [among whom Gibbon includes "the elder Brutus"] . . . excite the warmest Sensations of Esteem and Gratitude in those breasts which feel for the interest of Mankind. But the Design of the younger Brutus was vast and perhaps impracticable, the Execution feeble and unfortunate. Neither as a Statesman nor as a General did Brutus ever approve himself equal to the arduous task he had so rashly undertaken, of restoring the Commonwealth; instead of restoring it, the Death of a mild and generous Usurper produced only a series of Civil Wars, and the Reign of three Tyrants whose union and whose discord were alike fatal to the Roman People.

The sagacious Tully often laments that he could be pleased with nothing in the Ides of March, except the Ides themselves; that the Deed was executed with a manly Courage, but supported by childish counsels; that the Tyranny survived the Tyrant; as the Conspirators, satisfied with Fame and Revenge, had neglected every Measure that might have restored public Liberty. Whilst Brutus and Cassius contemplated their own Heroism with the most happy Complacency, Marc Antony who had preserved his Life, and the first Magistracy of the State by their injudicious clemency, seized the Papers and Treasure of the Dictator, inflamed the People and the Veterans, and drove them out of Rome and Italy, without any other Opposition than some grave Remonstrances which the Patriots vainly addressed to the Consul.[1]

Gibbon is of course speaking of the "historical" Brutus, but everything he says applies with at least equal force to Shakespeare's Brutus. Shakespeare has Brutus make all the mistakes Gibbon lists, and others. Moreover, just as Gibbon in answer to his own question says Brutus' virtue consisted in his disinterested intention,[2] so Shakespeare reworks his source materials so that Brutus' concern for pure intentions becomes the decisive cause of the conspirators' major errors and defeat. Yet Shakespeare's Brutus, like his historical model, enjoys the highest

1. "Digression on the Character of Brutus," in *The English Essays of Edward Gibbon*, ed. Patricia B. Craddock (Oxford: Clarendon Press, 1972), 96f.
2. *Ibid.*, 98.

esteem and respect for his virtue. Nearly everyone in the play loves or admires him:[3]

> O, he sits high in all the people's hearts;
> And that which would appear offence in us
> His countenance, like richest alchemy,
> Will change to virtue and to worthiness.
> (I.iii.157–160)

Cassius bows to his judgment out of love and respect for his "noble mind" (I.ii.308). Portia loves him dearly and looks up to him as the model Roman. Caius Ligarius considers him the "Soul of Rome" and pledges to do anything, even "things impossible," if only Brutus leads him (II.i.321–325). Lucilius gladly risks life and honor for him, and Brutus' defeated soldiers finally measure their own worth by how devotedly they served him. Even his enemies honor him highly. Octavius pays his virtue last respects, and Antony's final words laud his disinterested motives:

> This was the noblest Roman of them all.
> All the conspirators save only he
> Did that they did in envy of great Caesar;
> He only,[4] in a general honest thought
> And common good to all, made one of them.
> His life was gentle, and the elements
> So mix'd in him, that Nature might stand up
> And say to all the world, "This was a man!"
> (V.v.68–75)

To most Shakespearean critics, too, Brutus seems the perfect idea of Roman virtue. Mungo MacCallum, perhaps the play's most respected and influential 20th Century critic, expresses a conclusion shared by many. While stressing that Shakespeare actually "heightens the folly" of Brutus' mistakes by altering Plutarch's

---

3. E. A. J. Honigmann, *Shakespeare: Seven Tragedies* (New York: Harper and Row, 1976), 42f.
4. The Arden edn., like most recent edns., follows the Quarto (1691). The usually authoritative First Folio reads, "He, onely . . ." In a sense both are right. Properly speaking, "only" does double duty here, modifying what precedes it and what follows it.

account so as to point up his Stoic intentions, MacCallum never-theless argues that the playwright "screens from view whatever in the career of Brutus might prejudice his claims to our affection and respect." Indeed, while "to Plutarch Brutus is, so to speak, the model republican, the paragon of private and civic virtue," to Shakespeare, MacCallum believes, he is even more. Plutarch reports that

> Brutus in a contrary manner [to Cassius], for his virtue and
> valiantness, was well-beloved of the people and his own,
> esteemed of noble men, and hated of no man, not so much as
> of his enemies, because he was a marvelous lowly and
> gentle person, noble minded, and would never be in any rage,
> nor carried away with pleasure and covetousness, but had
> ever an upright mind with him, and would never yield to any
> wrong or injustice, the which was the chiefest cause of his
> fame, of his rising, and of the good will that every man bore
> him; for they were all persuaded that his intent was good.[5]

Shakespeare, "adopt[ing] and purif[ying]" this conception of Brutus, "carries much further [the] process of idealization that Plutarch had already begun."[6] In MacCallum's eyes, neither Rome's defeat, nor Brutus' heightened folly in contributing to that defeat, detracts from his stature as the paragon of civic as well as private virtue.[7]

Impressed by his Stoic principles, even the best critics have taken Brutus' republicanism for granted. Although recognizing something ambiguous about his virtue, Allan Bloom's interpreta-

---

5. *Brutus*, 29.2–3; *Shakespeare's Plutarch*, ed. W. W. Skeat (London: Macmillan and Co., 1875), 129.
6. *Shakespeare's Roman Plays and Their Background* (London: Macmillan and Co., 1967), 249, 234, 233.
7. Edward Dowden (*Shakespeare: His Mind and Art* [3rd edn.] [New York: Harper and Brothers, n.d.] 249), an important 19th Century critic, goes further:

> In *Julius Caesar* Shakespeare makes a complete imaginative study of the case of a man predestined to failure, who, nevertheless retains to the end the moral integrity which he prized as his highest possession, and who with each new error advances a fresh claim upon our admiration and our love.

Consider also Nietzsche, *Joyful Wisdom*, 98.

tion of *Caesar* rests squarely on the traditional view that "virtue, to [Brutus], is incorporated in the life of a good citizen."[8]

> The motivation of both Brutus and Cassius are truly republican, with the difference that, according to the formula of the time, the one hated tyranny, and the other, tyrants. . . . Both positions reflect elements in the republican character; the one presents the principles, the other, the passions which must be combined for a republican regime to endure. . . . Both Brutus and Cassius are noble Romans, the sort of men who made republican Rome the glory of political history.[9]

Yet Brutus' patriotism is not so unproblematical. His Stoic ethics of intention, depending on an opposition between self-interest and duty, proves to contain an antirepublican disdain for the success of his own political cause and even for the welfare of his country. Far from representing the principles of republican Rome, Brutus' celebrated virtue is, on the contrary, at once a reflection of and a reaction to the rise of imperial Rome.[10]

The first three sections of this essay will concentrate on the meeting at Brutus' house shortly before Caesar's assassination, when the conspiracy's intended moral figurehead becomes its political brains, as Brutus makes three important decisions against Cassius' better judgment: 1) not to swear an oath of resolution, 2) not to include Cicero in the plot, and 3) not to kill Antony along with Caesar. The last two sections will then consider Brutus' notion of the general good and the specific connection between his virtue and the rise of imperial Rome.[11]

---

8. *Shakespeare's Politics*, 92. Bloom sees the problem of Brutus' virtue not in terms of its antirepublicanism but rather in terms of his hypocritical refusal to acknowledge the necessary conditions of his high-minded virtue; see *ibid.*, 96ff.

9. *Ibid.*, 94.

10. Paul A. Cantor (*Shakespeare's Rome* [Ithaca: Cornell Univ. Press, 1976]), while offering an excellent discussion of the connection between imperial Rome and the ethics of intention (145–154), follows Bloom in taking for granted that Brutus' virtue is essentially republican or public spirited (37f.). Cantor, in other words, fails to see the basic similarity between the apparent moral opposites, Brutus and Antony.

11. Recent studies of Brutus' Stoicism include Marvin L. Vawter, " 'Division 'tween Our Souls': Shakespeare's Stoic Brutus," *Shakespeare Studies,* Vol. 7 (1974), 173–195, and Ruth M. Levitsky, " 'The Elements Were So Mix'd . . .' " *PMLA,* Vol. 88, No. 2 (March 1973), 240–245.

1.

The conspirators arrive at Brutus' house with "their hats . . . pluck'd about their ears, / And half their faces buried in their cloaks" (II.i.73–74). Although the night is so unusually bright that he can read without a candle (44–45), Brutus immediately assumes the conspirators' concealment is a sign of shame. His strong aversion to stealth, which seems of a piece with his devotion to the common good, leads him to believe they are ashamed to show their faces even "by night, / When evils are most free" (78–79). He regards their concealment not as a reasonable precaution in the pursuit of an honorable cause, but as a tacit confession that their cause is unjust. Justice, he believes, is public in every respect, and thus he considers the cloaked conspirators merely a "faction" (77). Their partial appearance betokens a partisan purpose. This moral revulsion to their covert activity is emblematic of his political decisions.

Brutus asks the other conspirators to give him their "hands over all, one by one." But when Cassius then proposes they "swear [their] resolution," Brutus immediately objects.

> No, not an oath. If not the face of men,
> The sufferance of our souls, the time's abuse—
> If these be motives weak, break off betimes,
> And every man hence to his idle bed.
> So let high-sighted tyranny range on,
> Till each man drop by lottery. But if these,
> As I am sure they do, bear fire enough
> To kindle cowards and to steel with valour
> The melting spirits of women, then, countrymen,
> What need we any spur but our own cause
> To prick us to redress? what other bond
> Than secret Romans, that have spoke the word,
> And will not palter? and what other oath
> Than honesty to honesty engag'd,
> That this shall be, or we will fall for it?
> Swear priests and cowards, and men cautelous,
> Old feeble carrions, and such suffering souls
> That welcome wrongs; unto bad causes swear
> Such creatures as men doubt; but do not stain
> The even virtue of our enterprise,

> Nor th' insuppressive mettle of our spirits,
> To think that or our cause or our performance
> Did need an oath; when every drop of blood,
> That every Roman bears, and nobly bears,
> Is guilty of a several bastardy,
> If he do break the smallest particle
> Of any promise that hath pass'd from him.
> (114–140)

Brutus' spirited objection presents a manly challenge: those needing to swear their resolution lack even the strength of women. His first decision is thus often praised for expressing republican sentiments. For example, Norman Rabkin, calling him "the ardent republican, the ideal Roman," argues that

> Brutus is right. What good is an oath which merely ornaments an action conceived in honor and love of country? Moreover, he is right practically. Any member of the band so inclined could break the oath to his own advantage and warn Caesar, but none does so in the absence of an oath. Oaths then are meaningless.[12]

Rabkin may have a point, but it is not Brutus'. Brutus objects not because a sworn oath would be superfluous, but for the opposite reason. He objects because swearing would be meaningful. Because it compels obedience, swearing an oath would "stain" the conspirators' "motives" and give the assassination the wrong meaning. The conspirators must do nothing that would belie virtue as their only concern.

Brutus' veto rests on a crucial distinction between a sworn oath, i.e., one sworn to the gods, and an oath exchanged among the conspirators, which, witnessed by no one save the "secret Romans" themselves, consists entirely in the integrity of their word. He objects to the former in the name of the latter because he considers swearing a sign of "need" (cp. 123 and 137). Brutus believes that virtuous men practice virtue for its own sake and not

---

12. *Shakespeare and the Common Understanding* (New York: Free Press, 1967), 108f.

for the sake of its extrinsic consequences. Such men therefore need nothing but their virtue to spur their action. Since their virtue is unconditional, they do their duty because it is right, not because it is compulsory. Swearing an oath, however, suggests just the opposite, that the actors' resolution depends on outside compulsion or supports. By calling upon the powerful gods to witness our oaths, swearing enforces our promises through fear of divine punishment for perjury. A sworn oath is thus a sign of moral weakness, for, rather than pledging the strength we have, it provides the strength we need. To suggest that the conspirators swear an oath is, then, to "think" that they "did need" one. It is to "stain" their "virtue" by doubting their "motives."[13]

2.

The second decision enlarges upon the rationale of the first.[14] Cassius asks whether they should sound out Cicero, adding that he thinks he will stand very strong with them. Several others agree, including Metellus Cimber:

> O, let us have him, for his silver hairs
> Will purchase us a good opinion,
> And buy men's voices to commend our deeds.
> It shall be said his judgment rul'd our hands;
> Our youths and wildness shall no whit appear,
> But all be buried in his gravity.
> (144–149)

---

13. Ernest Schanzer to the contrary notwithstanding (*The Problem Plays of Shakespeare* [New York: Schocken Books, 1965] 46), Shakespeare alters Plutarch's account of Brutus to give central importance to his ethics of intention and its political effects. In Plutarch nothing is said about Brutus' role in the first decision (or even that a decision, strictly speaking, was taken); the issue is not the conspirators' ability to maintain their "resolution" but to keep their "secret"; furthermore, "having never taken oaths together, nor taken or given any caution or assurance, nor binding themselves one to another by any religious oaths," they do not forswear a religious oath in the interests of another, purer sort of oath (*Brutus*, 12.6; Skeat, *Shakespeare's Plutarch*, 114). Note that the conspirators' meeting as a whole is Shakespeare's invention.

14. Critics have failed to see the relation between the first decision and those that follow, or even that they are related. Either approving or simply ignoring the first decision while generally criticizing the others, they misjudge its significance because, like Rabkin, they look to the wrong sort of evidence. The question is not whether the conspirators need to swear an oath, but why Brutus insists they prove they do not. His insistence, not their resolution, is the real issue. By recognizing this, we can see that the three decisions are in fact a concatenation.

But Brutus quickly vetoes the proposal:

> O, name him not; let us not break with him;
> For he will never follow any thing
> That other men begin.
> (150–152)

One important effect of this decision is to deprive the conspiracy of Cicero's vast rhetorical abilities. As Bloom remarks, it is hard to believe that the man universally acknowledged the greatest orator in Roman history would not have presented the reasons for the assassination at Caesar's funeral better than Brutus did.[15] However, the issue of Cicero's rhetoric is subordinate to the issue of his "judgment." Brutus rejects including Cicero because he objects to prudence on principle.

For Brutus, his rivalry with Cicero involves not only who will be the conspiracy's acknowledged leader, but also, and especially, what "shall be said" to have "rul'd [the assassins'] hands." Brutus knows that both would add respectability to the plot, but each for opposite virtues: Brutus for the purity of his intentions, Cicero for the prudence of his judgment.[16]

According to Brutus' conception of virtue, since virtue is voluntary, an action possesses no moral significance except insofar as it is voluntary. Its moral element therefore lies wholly within its initial inception or inward prompting—what Brutus calls "the first motion" (64)—and not in its ultimate outcome or outward consequence. It rests in the actor's will or intention, not the the action's results. The actor's motives are thus the sole standard for judging the justice of an action. Standing above its outcome, virtue consists in choosing the right end rather than in achieving it, in aiming straight rather than in hitting the target. Moreover, since virtue is a disposition or attitude of the mind, it does not require knowledge. Exclusive regard for intention makes judgment superfluous while making justice inherently good.[17]

---

15. *Shakespeare's Politics*, 98; also MacCallum, *Shakespeare's Roman Plays*, 249.

16. Here I borrow from Bloom (*Shakespeare's Politics*, 98) where a similar formulation is used. Bloom, however, sees Brutus' imprudence not as a matter of principle but as the unwitting result of his rashness and hypocrisy; see *ibid.*, 92–101.

17. See esp. Cicero, *De Finibus*, III.

Prudence, on the other hand, is essentially instrumental. While presupposing a moral purpose, it deals directly with means rather than with ends. As Metellus Cimber's unfortunate metaphor of commerce signifies, it is always exercised for the sake of an end outside its own activity and not simply for its own sake.[18] Cassius is correct when he reminds Brutus:

> Of your philosophy you make no use,
> If you give place to accidental evils.
> (IV.iii.144–145)

But whereas Stoic wisdom patiently endures such evils,[19] prudence is concerned with carefully avoiding them. To follow its counsels is therefore tantamount to conceding that virtue is not the only good or perhaps even the highest good and that happiness is indeed affected by things independent of one's will. It amounts to acknowledging that virtue is neither selfless nor self-sufficient, that its practice includes a consideration of extrinsic consequences and depends on the support of external goods.

Brutus rejects Cicero, then, for essentially the same reason he rejected swearing an oath. To be ruled by Cicero's "judgment" is to "make no use" of his own "philosophy."[20] The second decision goes beyond the first, however, in pointing up how concerned Brutus is with what others will say or think about his motives. An honorable reputation is as important to him as to any other Roman. But whereas a more traditional Roman would seek honor for his beneficial actions, Brutus seeks fame and glory for his honorable motives. Brutus, whose character in part combines personal ambition and selfless principles, fears that the reputation "the sagacious Tully" would lend the conspiracy would compromise the one he

---

18. Aristotle, *Nicomachean Ethics*, 1112b12ff.

19. I.ii.137–139; IV.iii.66–69, 189–191; V.i.101–108.

20. Stoicism differs from Aristotle's teaching in regarding moral virtue as the highest good and consequently in making moral choice the final as well as the efficient cause of action. It differs from Kant's teaching, on the other hand, in considering the moral life to be the life according to nature and in holding that the virtuous man is always happy.

seeks for himself.[21] The third decision will show how far he is prepared to go to avoid the compromising appearance of prudence.

3.

Decius next raises the question of whether only Caesar should be killed, and Cassius, thinking to events beyond the assassination, urges that Antony should also fall lest in sparing him the conspirators in effect save Caesar. But Brutus objects. His objection, however, has almost nothing to do with Antony. It is concerned instead with how the conspirators' motives for killing Caesar will appear. "Our course will seem too bloody, Caius Cassius," he explains,

> To cut the head off and then hack the limbs,
> Like wrath in death and envy afterwards;
> For Antony is but a limb of Caesar.
> Let's be sacrificers, but not butchers, Caius.
> We all stand up against the spirit of Caesar,
> And in the spirit of men there is no blood.
> O, that we then could come by Caesar's spirit,
> And not dismember Caesar! But, alas,
> Caesar must bleed for it. And, gentle friends,
> Let's kill him boldly, but not wrathfully;
> Let's carve him as a dish fit for the gods,
> Not hew him as a carcass fit for hounds.
> And let our hearts, as subtle masters do,
> Stir up their servants to an act of rage,
> And after seem to chide 'em. This shall make
> Our purpose necessary, and not envious;
> Which so appearing to the common eyes,
> We shall be call'd purgers, not murderers.
> And for Mark Antony, think not of him;
> For he can do no more than Caesar's arm
> When Caesar's head is off.
> (162–183)

---

21. In Plutarch (*Brutus*, 12.1–2; *Cicero*, 42.1) the conspirators as a group, not Brutus alone in opposition to their collective judgment, decide to exclude Cicero, and not because of his unwillingness to follow another's lead but because they fear his natural timidity, increased by age, would blunt the edge of their ardor at a crisis demanding speed.

Brutus' opposition springs from a paramount concern for the conspirators' reputation, not their eventual success. Killing Antony, he fears, would cause them to be "call'd" the wrong thing because the additional violence would give the wrong impression of their "purpose" for killing Caesar.

Critics often point out that Brutus, unable to permit himself full consciousness of what he is doing, tries to transform Caesar's assassination into something it is not. He tries to purify the deed of any taint of butchery by raising it to the level of pious sacrifice.[22] He attempts this, however, not to cloak the deed with false appearances, but so the truth can be seen. The assassination must seem to be exactly what it is. Insisting on moral transparency, he demands that the assassination be performed in such a way as will show that the killers' "purpose" was "necessary, and not envious." Their actions must assure "the common eyes" that their intention was free from any interested or passionate motive.

Imitating the indirect ways of "subtle masters," the conspirators must show that their hearts were not in their action, that Caesar's death was nothing but a reluctant concession to justice. They must therefore not only act dispassionately and limit the violence by sparing Antony; they must also seem reluctant to kill Caesar, for reluctance, even more than dispassion, attests to disinterestedness. Reluctance to do their duty will show that their action was prompted by nothing but their duty—a paradox that helps explain why Brutus, although very careful to conceal his internal torments after deciding to kill Caesar, is willing, even eager, to let others see how painful it was for him to choose public duty over personal friendship.

But Brutus knows that protests of reluctance, while important, are not enough. "Though now we must appear bloody and cruel," he explains to Antony after Caesar's death,

---

22. E.g., Bloom, *Shakespeare's Politics*, 96; Brents Stirling, *Unity in Shakespearean Tragedy* (New York: Columbia Univ. Press, 1956), 46.

> As by our hands and this our present act
> You see we do, yet see you but our hands
> And this the bleeding business they have done.
> Our hearts you see not; they are pitiful;
> And pity to the general wrong of Rome—
> As fire drives out fire, so pity pity—
> Hath done this deed on Caesar.
> (III.i.165–172)

Because men tend to judge intentions by results, it is most important to Brutus that Caesar's death promise the assassins no personal gain. Others, including Caesar's partisans, may benefit, but not the assassins (III.ii.42–48). Their action, in fact, must entail a deep and conspicuous personal loss. The sacrifice of his "best lover" shows that Brutus acted "for the good of Rome" (III.ii.46). "Not that I loved Caesar less, but that I loved Rome more." (III.ii.22–23) What men give up, not what they gain, shows their disinterestedness. Accordingly, when Cassius says he still fears Antony "For the ingrafted love he bears to Caesar," Brutus replies,

> Alas, good Cassius, do not think of him:
> If he love Caesar, all that he can do
> Is to himself: take thought, and die for Caesar.
> (II.i.184–187)

Men's loves are measured by their losses. The purity of a man's intentions is best shown by the sacrifice of what he holds most dear. As the purity of an act is best revealed by its imprudence, the ethics of intention, disdaining prudence, ultimately courts political defeat.[23]

---

23. In Plutarch Brutus does not spare Antony for the sake of how the assassins' motives will appear. Moreover, his naivete has a different quality there from what it has in Shakespeare. Plutarch reports that all the conspirators except Brutus thought Antony should be killed because he was wicked and naturally favored monarchy, was held in high esteem by the soldiers, and, particularly, because in addition to a mind bent to great actions he also had the great authority of the consulship, being then consul with Caesar.

> But Brutus would not agree to it. First, for he said it was not honest; secondly, because he told them there was hope of change in him. For he did not mistrust but that Antonius, being a noble-minded and courageous man (when he should know that Caesar was dead) would willingly help his country to recover her liberty, having them as an example to him, to follow their courage and virtue. (*Brutus*, 18.2–3; Skeat, *Shakespeare's Plutarch*, 119f.)

4.

Brutus' conception of the general good lacks a public or republican spirit. Before the conspirators arrive at his house, Brutus, having deliberated alone all night, reviews the considerations that led him to conclude Caesar must be killed. His speech begins,

> It must be by his death: and for my part,
> I know no personal cause to spurn at him,
> But for the general.
> (II.i.10–12)

Brutus affirms (as any republican might) that he will act for the sake of the general good. But what he means by "the general" is unrelated to republicanism.[24] His Stoic soliloquy is devoid of considerations of republican freedom, honor, and tradition. In it, he

---

Whereas in Plutarch Brutus expects a virtuous example to have a virtuous effect on the "noble-minded" Antony, in Shakespeare he dismisses him as politically harmless because he considers him morally despicable (II.i.185–190). In Plutarch he expects too much; in Shakespeare, too little. In both accounts he believes that strength comes from virtue, but in Shakespeare he believes that vice renders a man negligible in every respect while in Plutarch he believes that even a man like Antony can be "noble-minded and courageous." In sparing Antony, Shakespeare's Brutus seems at once more naive and less generous than his historical model.

We should also note that Shakespeare makes Brutus' most notorious blunder—agreeing to arrange Caesar's funeral as Antony would have it—merely the culmination of his previous decisions. Brutus agrees to Antony's proposal so he can "show the reason of our Caesar's death" (III.i.237). By "show," however, he means to demonstrate by action as well as to tell. He offers Antony the last word at the funeral (III.i.226–252) and then begs the crowd to stay and listen (III.ii.57–63), not so much because he thinks he will give unanswerable reasons for Caesar's death, but because he wants to demonstrate his disinterestedness by allowing Caesar's loyal partisan to speak. As least as important to him as what he will say is that both he and Antony will announce that Antony speaks by the assassins' permission (III.i.235–251; III.ii.56–63, 83–85). Antony does indeed speak "For Brutus' sake" (III.ii.58, 67). By allowing Antony to praise their victim's glories, the conspirators will show their honorable motives. See the text at n. 33 below.

For an excellent discussion of how Shakespeare modifies Plutarch's account both to make Brutus' "responsibility" for the error "undivided" and to remove "all the explanatory circumstances" for the decision, see MacCallum, *Shakespeare's Roman Plays*, 249f. Note also that Shakespeare even takes from Plutarch Antony's cunning reason to bury Caesar honorably and gives it to Brutus (Algeron de Vivier, "Julius Caesar," in *Shakespearean Studies*, ed. Matthews and Thorndike [New York, 1916; rpt. New York: Russell and Russell, 1962], 261).

24. Saying he does not see "in what point of view [Shakespeare] meant Brutus' character to appear" in this soliloquy, Coleridge (*Lectures and Notes on Shakespeare* [London: George Bell and Sons, 1908], 313) remarks that "surely nothing can seem more discordant with our historical preconceptions of Brutus, or more lowering to the intellect of the Stoico-Platonic tyrannicide, than the tenets here attributed to him—to him, the stern republican." Note that the soliloquy is Shakespeare's invention.

never equates monarchy and tyranny; he shows no shame at living in awe of an equal; and while ignoring the sacred oath his ancestor made the Romans swear never to tolerate another king in Rome, he expresses readiness to accept Rome's return to monarchy providing only that reason continue to rule the king monarchically. Perhaps most telling, he never even mentions Rome.

What Brutus means by "the general good" is indicated by the way in which he begins the speech. Focusing on his own "part," he denies any "personal cause" against Caesar. He sees dedication to the general good in terms of the motives for, not the results of, his actions. Brutus thus confuses impartiality with public-spiritedness. His failure to recognize a middle ground between base self-interest and noble self-sacrifice leads him to believe that sacrificing his own private satisfaction is the same as serving the public good. Brutus is thus dedicated to the general good chiefly in the negative sense of being willing to accept self-sacrifice, but not in the positive sense of actually benefiting his country. As is true of Stoicism in general, his virtue is related principally to enduring evils, not to bestowing goods.

To be sure, Brutus also wishes to live up to his illustrious name and emulate his revered ancestor, Junius Brutus, the founder of Rome's liberties. This is the side of him that Cassius appeals to when trying to arouse his republicanism to overcome his Stoic patience:

> O, you and I have heard our fathers say,
> There was a Brutus once that would have brook'd
> Th' eternal devil to keep his state in Rome
> As easily as a king.
> (I.ii.156–159)

And Cassius' efforts have an effect best seen in Brutus' patriotic response to his anonymous note:

> Shall Rome stand under one man's awe? What, Rome?
> My ancestors did from the streets of Rome
> The Tarquin drive, when he was call'd a king.

> "Speak, strike, redress!" Am I entreated
> To speak, and strike? O Rome, I make thee promise,
> If the redress will follow, thou receivest
> Thy full petition at the hand of Brutus.
> (II.i.52–58)

All the republican considerations missing from his Stoic deliberations are present here. Far from tolerating a king in Rome providing the king could remain virtuous, Brutus is now unwilling to endure Rome's standing under "one man's awe" under any conditions. The issue is no longer the overthrow of monarchy in Caesar, but of republicanism in Rome. Accordingly, Brutus does not present himself as Rome's disinterested arbiter, standing dispassionately over his country's fate. Instead, imagining himself petitioned by Rome, he pledges himself to an apostrophized Rome and, in further contrast to his Stoic soliloquy, emphasizes his own hand in the promised action. Whereas in the other speech he never mentions Rome, in this one (II.i.46–58) he mentions Rome as many times as in the rest of his lines combined.[25] What matters to him now is Rome's redress, not his own motives. Concern for his country's well-being replaces concern for the purity of his own intentions.[26] Cassius' republican instigations, however, have only a short-lived effect. The conspirators soon arrive, and Brutus' civic virtue gives way again to his Stoicism.[27] Without constant prodding, his virtue lacks a genuine public dimension. Nowhere is this more apparent than at the end of his life.

Although he seems willing to sacrifice every personal good to the common good, what Brutus finally sacrifices is not so much him-

---

25. Brutus mentions Rome twelve times altogether, six in these thirteen lines. This soliloquy is also the only speech in the play to begin and end with the speaker's name.

26. In *Lucrece,* Junius Brutus is so contemptuous of the wish to show pure intentions that he criticizes not only Lucrece's soft husband, Collatine, for not revenging her rape, but Lucrece as well for killing herself to prove her "mind" was "pure" (1. 1704): "Why Collatine, is woe the cure for woe? / Do wounds help wounds, or grief help grievous deeds? / Is it revenge to give thyself a blow / For his foul act by whom thy fair wife bleeds? / Such childish humour from weak minds proceeds; / Thy wretched wife mistook the matter so, / To slay herself that should have slain her foe." (11. 1821–1827) Republican Rome might be said to combine the qualities of Junius Brutus and Lucrece.

27. Note that Brutus' three decisions are decreasingly republican. The first contains his only mention of tyranny (II.i.118).

self as his country. Brutus says he knows "no personal cause" to act against Caesar. And at Caesar's funeral, just as he argues that the sacrifice of a dear friend shows that he killed Caesar for the good of Rome, so he also declares his willingness to kill himself for that cause: "as I slew my best lover for the good of Rome, I have the same dagger for myself, when it shall please my country to need my death." (III.ii.26–28) But Brutus does not die for his country, or even thinking of his country. His thoughts center on himself as he prepares to die, and he judges his life by a standard wholly unconnected with "the good of Rome."

> Countrymen,
> My heart doth joy that yet in all my life
> I found no man but he was true to me.
> I shall have glory by this losing day
> More than Octavius and Mark Antony
> By this vile conquest shall attain unto.
> So fare you well at once; for Brutus' tongue
> Hath almost ended his life's history.
> Night hangs upon mine eyes; my bones would rest,
> That have but labour'd to attain this hour.
> (V.v.33–42)

Brutus says he has labored his whole life only "to attain this hour." But his hour of triumphant "glory" is also his country's "losing day." What he has striven his entire life to attain stands apart from, or above, the downfall of his country. His personal moral victory shines through and eclipses the "vile conquest" of Rome herself. Similarly, just as his decisions as the conspiracy's leader are made not with a view to the political results of the conspirators' actions but with a view to the rectitude of their intentions, so too, running upon his sword, his dying thought is not of Rome or of the effects of his actions but of the goodness of his will:

> Caesar, now be still;
> I kill'd not thee with half so good a will.
> (V.v.50f.)

In the end, Brutus' ethics of intention, rather than extending his view to the whole community, narrows his vision to a purely personal concern. He ultimately values the purity of his soul above the welfare of his country.

5.

Brutus heralds the rise of a postrepublican, apolitical or antipolitical moral virtue. His ethics of intention, reflecting the transition to or the emergence of imperial Rome, is essentially a sign of deep disenchantment. It marks a world in which political action and victory have lost their noble quality because political causes have lost their public character.

In the earlier days of the Republic, Romans strove for Rome's highest honors by competing with one another against her foreign enemies. In winning conquests for Rome, they also won honor and glory for themselves. Their private ambitions were at once served and ennobled by their public service. The public realm, linking together self-interest and duty, allowed men to rise above their merely private concerns while at the same time devoting themselves to something they could love as their own. By the time of *Caesar*, however, Rome's vast expansion had seriously diminished her public realm.

> When could they say, till now, that talk'd of Rome,
> That her wide walks encompass'd but one man?
> Now is it Rome indeed, and room enough,
> When there is in it but one only man.
> (I.ii.152–155)

Since actions derive their meaning chiefly from the causes they serve, Rome's "universal" empire (I.i.44) robs her political life of its ennobling spirit by reducing political causes to private causes. Only one man in *Caesar*—Young Cato—dies in battle for his country. And just as his appearance is largely unexpected, so, too, the standard others use for measuring his nobility is the action of a man who kills himself to show personal loyalty to a friend (V.iv.9–

11).[28] With this single exception, the Romans serve their various leaders rather than their country under their leaders and measure their own worth by what amounts to private "service to [their] master[s]" (see esp. V.v.53–67).

Brutus' ethics of intention is a reaction to this degradation of political life.[29] It attempts to show or to find nobility in a world in which political victories become "vile" because no political action or cause is any longer truly public. As opportunities for public action and hence noble victories diminish, nobility does not so much disappear as it comes to be viewed in a radically new light. The dignity of intention rises as the dignity of action falls. Rather than seen chiefly in terms of action, nobility becomes internalized and, thought to dwell wholly within the actor himself, is understood in separation from or opposition to political action.[30]

Brutus' conception of honor reflects this new light. Honor was traditionally thought to be primarily an external reward for virtuous actions. Volumnia can speak of Coriolanus' "deed-achieving honour" (*Cor.* II.i.161), i.e., the honor he achieved for his deeds.

28. Young Cato dies declaring himself "A foe to tyrants, and my country's friend" (V.iv.5), but it is unclear whether he is honored for his action or for "being Cato's son" (V.iv.9–11).

29. Consider Caius Ligarius, who regards Brutus as the "Soul of Rome" (II.i.321) and is the only character to look to him from the start to lead the conspiracy. Ligarius, a "mortified spirit" (II.i.324) who almost literally embodies the ethics of intention, suffers an unjust fate which shows what his limited actions could not show—that he is too noble to live at Caesar's continued sufferance. While accompanying Brutus to Caesar's house, he does not proceed to the Senate and so has no hand in the deed for which the mob punishes him; II.i.215–220, 310–334; II.ii.111–113; III.iii.35–38.

30. For the difference between the pagan hero and the Christian hero or martyr ("witness"), see Augustine, *The City of God*, X.21. Among many allusions throughout *Caesar* to the coming of Christianity with its new sort of hero are the conversation immediately preceding Brutus' first decision in which "the high east" is said to stand directly beyond the Capitol (II.i.101–111); Decius' interpretation of Calphurnia's purported dream concerning Caesar's death, in which, as Samuel Johnson (1765) says, "There are two allusions: one to coats armorial . . .; the other to martyrs. . . . The Romans, says Decius, all come to you, as to a saint, for reliques; as to a prince, for honours." (quoted by Dorsch, *Julius Caesar*, 55f.); and the number of Caesar's wounds, which in Plutarch, Suetonius and Appian are twenty-three but in Shakespeare thirty-three (V.i.53). (For the symbolic significance of this number in Shakespeare, see Howard B. White, *Copp'd Hills Toward Heaven: Shakespeare and the Classical Polity* [The Hague: Nijhoff, 1970], 75.) For other allusions, see Roy W. Battenhouse, *Shakespearean Tragedy* (Bloomington: Indiana Univ. Press, 1969), 92f.

No one would describe Brutus' honor in that way, least of all Brutus himself. Brutus begins his funeral oration by reminding the crowd of his honor:

> Romans, countrymen, and lovers, hear me for my cause, and be silent, that you may hear. Believe me for mine honour, and have respect to mine honour, that you may believe. (III.ii.13–16)

"Honour" here signifies a virtuous disposition, not a noble reward. It is the standard for judging rather than the recognition for performing a certain action. Like "honesty" (which is even more closely associated with Brutus), it is a virtue or virtuous motive rather than virtue's noblest effect; and, again like "honesty," it has the sense rather of abstaining from wrongdoing than of actually conferring benefits. Characteristically, Brutus believes that, if the people keep in mind that he is honorable, they will be convinced that Caesar's killing was just. Honorable motives by themselves make for an honorable deed. Since intentions are everything, the actions of an honorable man are just simply because he is honorable. They are and remain honorable whatever their consequences or success.[31]

Brutus' virtue also reflects Rome's emerging regime insofar as imperial Rome has no public life. It is especially fitting that Antony eulogizes Brutus for his disinterestedness, for even though Brutus considers him his moral opposite, Antony proves to epitomize the postrepublican notion that one can gain more by losing politically than by winning.[32] Brutus' virtuous self-denial is of a piece with

---

31. See Norman Council, *When Honour's at the Stake* (New York: Harper and Row, 1973), 60–74, and note esp. his remarks on Casca's alchemical metaphor at I.iii.157–160 (63).

The difference between the spirit of Brutus' virtue and republicanism is further indicated by the following Shakespearean revision. According to Plutarch, when Portia disclosed to Brutus that she had gashed herself in the thigh to prove herself worthy of his trust, "Brutus was amazed to hear what she said unto him, and lifting up his hands to heaven, he besought the goddess to give him the grace he might bring his enterprize to so good pass that he might be found a husband worthy of so noble a wife as Portia." (*Brutus*, 13.6; Skeat, *Shakespeare's Plutarch*, 116) In Shakespeare, Brutus, hearing of her proof, also prays to the gods to "Render me worthy of this noble wife!" but is silent about the success of the republican cause (II.i.302f.).

32. See Cantor, *Shakespeare's Rome*, 148ff.

Antony's sensual self-indulgence. They are the twin representatives of the new Rome. The one is duty, the other desire, separated from public concerns; and in imperial Rome, as we find in *Antony and Cleopatra,* there is "no midway / 'Twixt these extremes at all." (*A&C* III.iv.19–20) Characterized by a middle void, imperial Rome has nothing that can mediate between desire and duty.

Whereas citizen virtue, combining elements of "realism" and "idealism," adds nobility to self-interest and friendship or fraternity to justice, and in so doing both ennobles and moderates these two extremes, Brutus' virtue, recognizing only the noble and not the necessary as just, lacks moderation and ultimately even more. In the end it lacks humanity. If man is somehow connected to both what is above and what is below him, his humanity depends on recognizing these two aspects of his nature and giving each its due. It may even be that man is man by virtue of that middle ground or part of the soul that mediates between these extremes, for neither extreme is distinctly human; one is bestial, the other divine. Brutus shows he recognizes this, at least in some sense, when he fears that Caesar would sink to the level of the lowest beast if, upon reaching the highest rung of ambition's ladder, he thought himself a god (II.i.10–34). To remember one's humanity means to remember one's place "in between." But this is just what Brutus forgets in practicing a moral virtue that disdains political results.

There is something brutish about Brutus or his "idealism." As Caesar's last words to him suggest (III.i.77), in killing Caesar he does indeed manage to live up to his name, but in a way he never meant. When Antony demands to be told why Caesar was dangerous, Brutus answers,

> Or else were this a savage spectacle.
> Our reasons are so full of good regard,
> That were you, Antony, the son of Caesar,
> You should be satisfied.
> (III.i.223–226)

The assasssins' deed would be savage, he says, unless their reasons could overcome the natural love of one's own.[33] Yet it is in trying to demonstrate just such disinterestedness that Brutus proves to be truly brutish.

Moments after the assassination, he exhorts the killers:

> Stoop, Romans, stoop,
> And let us bathe our hands in Caesar's blood
> Up to the elbows, and besmear our swords:
> Then walk we forth, even to the market-place,
> And waving our red weapons o'ver our heads,
> Let's all cry, "Peace, freedom, and liberty!"
> (III.i.105–110)

This speech and the bloody ritual it ushers in remind us of Brutus' vain hope to kill Caesar without spilling his blood so that the conspirators' impersonal motives will be apparent to everyone. The speech and ritual are the solemn fulfillment of his wish to convert the assassination into a religious sacrifice. But what exactly does Brutus sacrifice? Unwilling to swear an oath to the gods lest it stain the conspirators' motives, he is willing to make the assassination a human sacrifice to the gods in order to demonstrate those motives. His moral idealism requires the barbaric sacrifice of human blood. Brutus expresses manly contempt for "such suffering souls / That welcome wrongs." Yet, unable to reconcile virtue and prudence, he ultimately pursues defeat. The defeat, however, is not his but Rome's. Unlike a soldier who sacrifices his own life for his country's victory, Brutus sacrifices the prospect of his country's victory for something entirely his own. Some Shakespearean critics, in important respects the spiritual heirs of postrepublican Rome, consider Brutus "the noblest Roman of them all" and admire him for prizing his ideals more than his country:

> The life of Brutus, as the lives of such men must be, was a
> good life, in spite of its disastrous fortunes. He had found
> no man who was not true to him. And he had known Portia.
> The idealist was predestined to failure in the positive world.

33. Hence Caesar's last words to Brutus in Suetonius, "And thou, my son?" (*Divus Julius*, 82) become "*Et tu, Brute?*" (III.i.77) in Shakespeare.

But for him true failure would have been disloyalty to his ideals. Of such failure he suffered none. Octavius and Mark Antony remained victors at Philippi. Yet the purest wreath of victory rests on the forehead of the defeated conspirator.[34]

But Shakespeare finds such idealism a degenerate form of nobility. Brutus' moral purity is his central moral as well as political defect. Rather than raise him to man's highest moral levels, his desire to place pure duty or justice over every ordinary human attachment finally degrades his humanity.

> O judgment, thou art fled to brutish beasts,
> And men have lost their reason.
> (III.ii.106–107)

The idealistic attempt to rise above every attachment to one's own proves in the end not to be a divine willingness to sacrifice one's own well-being for the sake of a higher good, but an inhuman willingness to sacrifice the welfare and happiness of those one seems selflessly to serve. Deprecating political results, Brutus ultimately disdains humanity.

---

34. Dowden, *Shakespeare*, 272.

Four

Caesar's Ambiguous End

DESPITE ITS APPARENT SIMPLICITY, CAESAR IS VERY AMBIGUOUS, PARTICU-larly in its presentation of Caesar.[1] Although dominating the world around him, the play's titular hero appears in only three scenes, speaks fewer than 150 lines, and is killed before the play is half over. Moreover, while his greatness is indisputably reflected in the men around him, in his influence over them and especially in the way they act in relation to him,[2] Caesar himself seems almost idle and much of what we see of him hardly measures up to what he says about himself. For example, he declares he is "as constant as the northern star" and as immovable as Mount Olympus soon after appearing indecisive about whether to attend the Senate; he

---

1. See Mungo MacCallum, *Shakespeare's Roman Plays and Their Background* (London: Macmillan and Co., 1967), esp. 218ff.; Ernest Schanzer, *The Problem Plays of Shakespeare* (New York: Schocken Books, 1965), 10ff.; Allan Bloom, *Shakespeare's Politics* (New York: Basic Books, 1964) 75f., 88−91.

2. Caesar is essentially right when he boasts, "The things that threaten'd me / Ne'er look'd but on my back; when they shall see / The face of Caesar, they are vanished." (II.ii.10−12) When Caesar first appears (I.ii.1−24) we see that Casca, who will stab him from behind, is the first to attend to his words; and although he jeers at Caesar behind his back (I.ii.231ff.), he is as obsequious as Antony to his face. Brutus, too, does his bidding, as does Cassius, his most resentful detractor, even though he complains bitterly in private that he "... must bend his body/If Caesar carelessly but nod on him." (I.ii.116f.) With the possible exception of Cicero, all of Caesar's republican enemies act one way in public and another in private. Caesar arrogates the prerogatives of at least a king, and all of Rome's nobles hold him in awe and pay him the deference he claims. See also V.i. 39−44.

asserts his superiority to every sort of adulation and blandishment when he appears to have been duped by Decius' flattery shortly before; and he claims to be absolutely fearless and even more dangerous than Danger itself only to seem to yield first to Calphurnia's fear for his safety and then to his own fear of what the senators might whisper about his courage were he to give way to her fear.[3] Shakespeare, it seems, has deliberately fashioned a Caesar who is at once great and small, victor and vanquished, triumphant hero and vainglorious fool. On the one hand, he is made to seem indecisive, insolent, self-deceiving, and petty; on the other, he is shown to be so much the master of the world that even the heavens reflect his image and herald his fall.

Caesar's ambiguity is hard to understand, and, not surprisingly, opposite interpretations abound.[4] As S. F. Johnson notes, "For some critics, Caesar is, in Antony's words, 'the noblest man / That ever lived in the tide of times' and the assassination a senseless act of criminal folly, while for others Caesar is an ambitious tyrant and the assassination a valiant attempt by patriotic Romans to preserve the Republic."[5] Most critics, however, whatever their differences in other respects, interpret Caesar's ambiguity as intended to show the final stage of decline of a once-great man. For example, H. M. Richmond, although recognizing "the superiority of Caesar's political instincts to those of all the men around him," concludes that "It is precisely the purely personal slackening of political acumen that Shakespeare has striven to evoke in his aging Julius Caesar—a portrait of decline drawn at the expense of strict fidelity to . . . Plutarch. . . ."[6] And Allan Bloom, although calling Caesar the greatest political man ever, argues,

---

3. II.ii.4–107, III.i.31–77.
4. See, e.g., John Dover Wilson, The New Shakespeare *Julius Caesar* (London: Cambridge Univ. Press, 1947), xxv, on the one side, and T. S. Dorsch, The Arden *Julius Caesar,* (London: Methuen, 1964), xxix, xxxviii–xxxix, and John Palmer, *Political Characters of Shakespeare* (London: Macmillan and Co., 1961), 35f., on the other.
5. *Julius Caesar* (New York: Penguin Books, 1976), 14.
6. *Shakespeare's Political Plays* (New York: Random House, 1967), 204.

. . . the real, live Caesar who confronts us is a man at the end
of his career. He has accomplished all he has to do. There
are few great actions left; he has only to reap vain honors. He
has triumphed over all possible opponents, and with a
certain sadness sees that his equals are no longer his equals. . . .
All that remains is the last forbidden fruit, the crown, the
opposition to which was the vital center of the Republic's
history. We see the glowing ashes of a Caesar who has been
consumed in his passion for glory. He is now indecisive and
prone to error. What is left is his own vision of what he
wanted to be and how he should be understood by others.

It would seem that Caesar, having "fulfilled the end implied in all
heroic ambition," has been robbed of his renowned political
judgment by his tremendous political success.[7]

Yet, while Caesar's actions are ambiguous, his ambition to
become a god is not.[8] And if his actions are examined with a view
to that ambition rather than to the commonly supposed ambition
to become king, they appear not only consistent but brilliantly
conceived and perfectly executed. They demonstrate characteristic
political traits that enabled Caesar to "get the start of the majestic
world, / And bear the palm alone" (I.ii.129f.)—his extraordinary
ability to beguile his enemies while flattering his supporters.

This essay will concentrate on the two scenes which are usually
thought to show Caesar at his worst, politically and
personally—Casca's report of what he did when Antony offered
him a crown at the Lupercal, and his appearance at home on the
morning of the ides when Decius comes to escort him to the
Capitol. We will see that what at first glance appear dull failures in
Caesar's attempt to become a king are in fact disguised successes in
his attempt to become a god. Caesar's actions, we will see, are

7. *Shakespeare's Politics*, 90, 75.
8. See esp. II.ii.44–48 and III.i.58–74. Although his essay begins, "*Julius Caesar* is the
story of a man who became a god" (*Shakespeare's Politics*, 75), Bloom does not develop this
theme. While pointing out that "Caesar conceives of himself as a god" (*ib.*, 90) and was in
fact "worshipped as a divinity, as were many of those who inherited his name" (*ib.*, 75), he
nonetheless judges his actions finally in terms of ambition for the crown.
For the fact that Caesar was ranked among the gods, not only by formal decree, but in the
belief of the people, see Suetonius, *Divus Julius*, 88.

designed to win him permanent fame and glory in the politically new world his achievements have brought about and whose implications he understands better than the men around him.

1.

Although Caesar's ambition is central to the play and, at least until the end of his funeral, uppermost on everyone's mind, Shakespeare does not allow us to see for ourselves what happens when Antony offers him a crown at the feast of Lupercal. Instead, he places this crucial episode offstage and presents it through Casca's report to Brutus and Cassius (I.ii.212–284). But Casca's report reveals as much about the republican Casca as about the antirepublican Caesar. By making us see Caesar's ambiguous actions through Casca's scornfully complacent eyes, Shakespeare shows us at once Caesar's extraordinary ability to manipulate the Roman people and his republican enemies' great difficulty in facing up to that threat. He presents the obvious corruption of Caesar's outrageous demagoguery through the subtle corruption of Casca's decaying republicanism.[9]

Casca, who is almost entirely Shakespeare's creation,[10] is probably the most traditional-minded republican in the play. Identifying the familiar with the good, he seems to take the Republic's continued existence for granted. His republicanism, like that of the common people he despises, has been undermined by his more basic attachment to the old or the customary as such. His republican virtue has thus degenerated largely into an attachment to traditional forms.[11] Casca's manly pride no longer

9. Typical of most interpretations is Dorsch's summary (*Caesar*, xxxi): "[Caesar] has been offered a crown, which of course he would like to accept; but he has felt compelled, or has felt it expedient, to refuse it, though three times offered. He is mortified by the applause that greeted his refusal. Moreover, he has made something of an exhibition of himself by being overcome by the stinking breath of the rabble and having an epileptic seizure."

10. All that Plutarch says is that Casca was the first to strike Caesar and struck him from behind, and that when Caesar cried out and gripped his hand, he shouted to his brother in Greek (*Caesar*, 66.4–5). Shakespeare includes the first but expressly rejects the second particular.

11. See chapt. 2, n. 27 above. Note that what terrifies Casca about the great storm in the next scene is not its destructive power but its complete novelty; its unfamiliarity arouses his deepest fears (I.iii.3–10).

inspires real citizen virtue. Rather than prompt him to defend the republican regime, it makes him content with merely distancing himself from its obvious corruption. Viewing his country's affairs with the detachment of an onlooker, he sees the final act of Rome's high drama mainly as a farce or burlesque.

The broad outline of his report seems simple enough, yet Casca himself in effect warns that it is incomplete:[12]

> I can as well be hang'd as tell the manner of it: it was mere foolery; I did not mark it.
> (231f.)

And the ensuing omissions, backtracking and revisions confirm that the events were not so simple as he would have his listeners first believe. "I saw Mark Antony offer him a crown," he begins,

> yet 'twas not a crown neither, 'twas one of these coronets;
> and, as I told you, he put it by once; but for all that, to my
> thinking, he would fain have had it. Then he offered it to him
> again; then he put it by again; but to my thinking, he was
> very loath to lay his fingers off it. And then he offered it the
> third time. He put it the third time by; and still as he
> refus'd it, the rabblement hooted, and clapp'd their chopt
> hands, and threw up their sweaty night-caps, and uttered
> such a deal of stinking breath because Caesar refus'd the
> crown, that it had, almost, choked Caesar; for he swounded,
> and fell down at it. And for mine own part, I durst not laugh,
> for fear of opening my lips and receiving the bad air.
> (232–247)

Casca is of course convinced Caesar's restraint was sham. He believes that Caesar, expecting to have his way with the people in this as in everything else, put Antony up to offering the crown and

---

12. Shakespeare seems to underscore the question of how reliable Casca's eyewitness report is by indicating that even our scant firsthand knowledge is less complete than first appears. We hear the crowd shout twice (I.ii.78, 120), and Shakespeare's stage directions call for only these two shouts. Yet Cassius says he heard three, and Casca, who was present, confirms that number (I.ii.222–240). In Plutarch (*Caesar* 61.3–4) the crown is offered twice.

refused it only because of the people's unexpected opposition. Describing Caesar's fall as the comically just culmination of his demagoguery, he suggests that Caesar was nearly asphyxiated by the shouts of approval for his doing exactly the opposite of what he wanted. But Casca's subsequent remarks show that he is by no means convinced Caesar fell involuntarily. When urged by the incredulous Cassius to say whether Caesar really swooned, Casca describes the incident again but this time without levity or explaining why he fell: "He fell in the market-place, and foam'd at mouth, and was speechless." (249f.) And when Brutus offers, " 'Tis very like; he hath the falling sickness" (251), Casca neither agrees nor disagrees, even though he will soon say that Caesar himself told the crowd "he desir'd their worships to think it was his infirmity" (267f.). All he says he is "sure" about is that

> Caesar fell down. If the tag-rag people did not clap him and hiss him, according as he pleas'd and displeas'd them, as they use to do the players in the theater, I am no true man. (254–258)

Casca, who evidently recognizes that there was something purely theatrical about Caesar's fall, also realizes—but chooses to suppress—that Caesar, far from suffering a mortifying fiasco, benefited from the whole affair and particularly from the fall. Brutus continues by asking, "What said he when he came unto himself?" (259) Since Casca seemed to give a complete account of everything up to Caesar's recovery, he might be expected to resume where he left off. But in order to explain what Caesar said afterwards, he first has to backtrack and add a significant part of the story he omitted from his original account—Caesar's histrionic offer of his life.

> Marry, before he fell down, when he perceiv'd the common herd was glad he refus'd the crown, he pluck'd me ope his doublet, and offer'd them his throat to cut. And I had been a man of any occupation, if I would not have taken him at a word, I would I might go to hell among the rogues. And so he fell. (260–266)

Instead of falling upon hearing the people's third shout (as Casca originally indicated), Caesar responded to their last shout by offering them "his throat to cut." His fall was immediately preceded not by their shout but by his astonishing offer. Casca's reluctance to reveal this is not surprising, for the fall's true context gives Caesar's actions as a whole a radically different meaning, one which makes it impossible to dismiss the episode as laughable demagoguery, harmful only to Caesar himself. What happened at the Lupercal may be reconstructed as follows. Caesar, having put Antony up to offering him a crown (as Casca suspects), first deliberately provoked the people's traditional opposition to a king by appearing "very loath to lay his fingers off it." But, after arousing their mounting opposition with each increasingly reluctant refusal, he terrified those he had just offended by offering them "his throat to cut" and then immediately compounded their frightened confusion by falling as though they had actually accepted his manly challenge and killed him for his proud ambition. Finally, having simulated his own assassination at their hands, he quickly reversed the effect and transformed their fear of ambition into virtually unbounded piteous forgiveness by telling them what "to think" about what they saw. "When he came to himself again," Casca continues,

> he said, if he had done or said anything amiss, he desir'd their worships to think it was his infirmity. Three or four wenches, where I stood, cried, "Alas, good soul," and forgave him with all their hearts; but there's no heed to be taken of them; if Caesar had stabb'd their mothers, they would have done no less.
> (266–272)

Casca recognizes but tries to slight that Caesar not only extricated himself easily from his apparent blunder, but, presenting himself to the people as a weak man, succeeded in enhancing his standing with them. The people were so taken in by what he did that the pity he aroused would have caused them to forgive him nearly anything.

Bloom argues that

> Finally, in seeking a crown and the title of king, [Caesar]
> seems guilty of imprudence. The people, who are serving
> under a monarch, do not wish to be aware of a situation
> which they themselves have created. Names mean every-
> thing to the people, and substance, nothing. Caesar appears to
> affront this sentiment unnecessarily, since he already holds
> all the real power of a king. There is something petty in his
> desire, however logical a consequence it may be of his own
> ambitions. It is the cause of the conspirators' final resolution.[13]

Caesar does indeed arouse the people's initial opposition and
provoke the conspirators' final resolution. But the lasting effect of
his actions is quite different from their initial effect. As Caesar's
contrived "fall" in the marketplace directly prefigures and
deliberately provokes his fatal "fall" in the Senate, so his
performance at the Lupercal, including his degrading display of
weakness, not only wins the people's piteous forgiveness but does
so in such a way as to provide them with an interpretation for his
death which later inspires them to worship him as a martyred
god.[14]

Despite his genuine disgust as a "true man," Casca is not stirred
to act by what he sees. Caesar's demagoguery arouses neither his
outrage nor his active concern for Rome.[15] Just as he makes up for
being obsequious to Caesar's face by jeering at him behind his
back,[16] so he generally contents himself with jesting at the

---

13. *Shakespeare's Politics*, 90.

14. The Lupercal episode is mostly Shakespeare's fabrication. In both Plutarch (*Caesar*, 61.3–4) and Shakespeare, Antony offers and Caesar refuses a crown at the festival of Lupercal. However, in Plutarch, Caesar's offer of "his throat to cut" does not occur at the Lupercal, is not made to the people, and has no connection with the offers and refusals of the crown. Plutarch says (*ib*. 60.3–4) Caesar made this offer on an earlier occasion after treating the senators like private persons. Aware that he had insulted them by not rising to receive them, Caesar pulled his toga from his neck and cried to his friends that he was ready to let anyone kill him who wanted to. Moreover, Plutarch does not say Caesar fell down, although Casca says so five times. Caesar's "fall" in the marketplace is in fact made up entirely by Shakespeare. In both accounts, Caesar uses his infirmity to excuse part of his behavior. But in Plutarch it is for his folly of not rising; in Shakespeare, for "anything amiss" he might have "done or said" when he fell.

15. Cassius later arouses him by appealing to a combination of his manly shame and fear of the unknown, while saying nothing about Caesar's demagoguery (I.iii.41 ff.).

16. Dorsch, *Caesar*, xxxii.

degrading basis of Caesar's success. The sight of Caesar's growing hold on the people encourages in him mostly the perverse satisfaction that he is above such corruption. He even scoffs at Caesar's silencing of the tribunes as another instance of the day's "foolery" (282–284). Yet his own account shows that if what happened at the Lupercal was indeed "mere foolery," it was so mainly in the sense that Caesar, the consummate master of simulation and dissimulation, completely fooled the people.[17]

2.

Just how well Caesar has played his part becomes evident· at his funeral when Antony, expressly reminding the people of what they all saw at the Lupercal, wins their reverence for him as a god by making them "feel / The dint of pity" (III.ii.195f.) for him as a man. No one can fail to be impressed by Antony's success. "If ever Shakespeare wished to show genius at work," writes T. S. Dorsch, "surely it was in Antony's oration." What particularly impresses many critics are the circumstances under which Antony speaks. "By a magnanimous and calmly reasonable appeal to their Roman sense of independence," Dorsch continues,

> Brutus has convinced an initially uneasy crowd that Caesar was an ambitious tyrant who had to be slain for the good of Rome, and they are ready to shower every honour on him as their deliverer. Antony is there on sufferance; he is to speak by the kind permission of the hero of the hour, and the crowd he faces is actively hostile to Caesar and likely to tear to pieces any one who exalts Caesar at the expense of Brutus.[18]

Similarly, Mungo MacCallum urges us to

> Consider the enormous difficulties of [Antony's] position. He is speaking under iimitation and by permission before a hostile audience that will barely give him a hearing, and his

---

17. Notwithstanding Brutus' description of him as "angry" and "sad" (I.ii.181,214), Caesar shows no displeasure with Antony or disappointment with the outcome of events at the Lupercal. Caesar knows one can "look / Quite through the deeds of men" (I.ii.199f.) because he is the perfect example.

18. *Caesar,* lii.

task is to turn them quite round, and make them adore what they hated and hate what they adored.[19]

Although Antony's circumstances are by no means easy, they are not so difficult as these remarks suggest. The people are ready to shower every honor on Brutus, but not because they see him as the defender of their political liberty or the savior of their country. And while Antony does have to face an audience that is initially disposed toward Brutus and no more than tolerant of him, he does not have to make them love what they hated and hate what they loved. It is in fact Brutus who attempts that, while Antony caters to what they already love and hate. Notwithstanding his shameless shamming and flagrant flattery, Antony is essentially correct when he assures the crowd, "I tell you that which you yourselves do know." (III.ii.226) His oration succeeds because it addresses itself entirely to Caesarian passions and principles and appeals directly to the interpretation Caesar has already suggested for his own death, while Brutus enjoys momentary success despite his republican appeal.[20]

Ambition is the only public charge brought against Caesar, the only reason publicly advanced for his death. Just as Brutus declares right after the assassination that "ambition's debt is paid"

---

19. *Shakespeare's Roman Plays,* 293.

20. Brutus ends his speech with a patriotic vow: "With this I depart, that, as I slew my best lover for the good of Rome, I have the same dagger for myself, when it shall please my country to need my death." (45–48) Whereas Brutus had to solicit the people's only previous response, which was meant to attest to their republican sentiments (35), the crowd's response now is both spontaneous and fervent: "Live, Brutus! live! live!" (49) Contrary to Brutus' expectations, a Roman's willingness to die for his country no longer elicits the people's respect for his virtue. It now excites chiefly their pity and fear for his fate. Brutus' oration apparently reminds at least one plebian of the Brutus who, more than four centuries earlier, had prevented the return of the kings to Rome. "Give him a statue with his ancestors," he cries (51). But, clearly, the people's remembrance of the Republic's origin and safeguard is incomplete. The same plebian who is "certain" Caesar was "a tyrant" and believes "We are blest that Rome is rid of him," also urges the people to "let [Brutus] be Caesar" (72, 52), while another declares, "Caesar's better parts / Shall be crown'd in Brutus." (52f.) Brutus' ancestors are only "his ancestors." They are no longer Rome's or the people's. And, to some people at least, Brutus deserves the highest honors precisely because of his resemblance to the man he killed.

(III.i.83), so he explains to the crowd at Caesar's funeral that "as [Caesar] was ambitious, I slew him" (III.ii.27). In accusing Caesar of ambition, Brutus appeals to one of the Roman people's oldest and deepest fears. While generally grateful to Rome's military heroes for victories in foreign wars, the Roman people were at the same time, and for the same reason, always fearful of them for their ambition in Rome's domestic strife. Even as they traditionally rewarded their conquering heroes with the city's highest civil honors, they nonetheless feared them becoming their own harsh oppressors. We see this clearly in *Coriolanus*. "Caius Marcius was / A worthy officer i' th' war," one of the tribunes acknowledges, "but," he continues,

> insolent,
> O'ercome with pride, ambitious past all thinking,
> Self-loving—

"And affecting one sole throne / Without assistance," his colleague concludes. (IV.vi.29–33) And so the people "banish [one of their] defenders" (III.ii.128) as his undisguised pride is readily made to appear to them a sign of his ambition for "Tyrannical power" (III.iii.2).[21] Unabashedly proud and ambitious and loving the common people far less than victory, Rome's heroes always aroused both fear and gratitude in the people, the one for the danger they posed, the other for the protection they provided. Brutus therefore tries to rally popular support for the assassination by arguing that Caesar was ambitious. "As Caesar loved me," he explains,

> I weep for him; as he was fortunate, I rejoice at it; as he was
> valiant, I honour him; but, as he was ambitious, I slew him.
> There is tears, for his love; joy, for his fortune; honour, for his
> valour; and death, for his ambition.
> (III.ii.18–29)

To the people, ambition is a capital crime.

---

21. See also *Coriolanus* V.ii.37ff., and cp. I.i.200ff.

Antony fully agrees that ambition deserves death. Near the beginning of his speech he reminds the crowd that

> The noble Brutus
> Hath told you Caesar was ambitious.
> If it were so, it were a grievous fault,
> And grievously hath Caesar answer'd it.
> (III.ii.79–82)

Yet Antony rather easily refutes Brutus' charge, largely by reminding the people of what they saw at the Lupercal:

> You all did see that on the Lupercal
> I thrice presented him a kingly crown,
> Which he did thrice refuse. Was this ambition?
> (97–99)

And a few moments later the same plebeian who had just urged the people to "crown" Caesar's better parts in Brutus (52f.) responds,

> Mark'd ye his words? He would not take the crown;
> Therefore 'tis certain he was not ambitious.
> (114f.)

The literal-minded people, equating the ambition to be king with ambition as such, readily believe that Caesar's spurning the crown is evidence he lacked ambition.

Antony makes no effort, however, to present Caesar's refusals in a republican light. On the contrary, his defense of Caesar is thoroughly antirepublican. Antony even goes so far as to remind everyone that it was he who thrice offered Caesar the "kingly crown." Whereas Brutus addresses the people as Roman citizens, appeals to patriotic sentiments and manly pride, honors Caesar for his valor, and demonstrates his own manly spirit by pledging his life to his country, Antony addresses them as private persons, appeals to their purely private concerns, urges reverence for Caesar's poverty, celebrates him for pitying the poor, and elicits the people's pity for himself by demonstrating his own pity for Caesar. Where Brutus speaks of loving Rome, Antony speaks of loving Caesar. And where

Brutus speaks of freedom and slavery and promises the people "a place in the commonwealth," Antony says nothing about freedom or slavery and promises them "common pleasures" instead (44f.,252). Thus, while Antony calls the assassins "traitors," their alleged "treason" is not said to have been committed against the city, the regime, or even the people as a class, but against the people and their protectors as private individuals (171–199). Antony's only considerations are entirely personal or private. Antony therefore repeatedly emphasizes men's most universal concerns, particularly the body and its needs, since the most universal concerns are also the most private. They pertain to men as men, not to men as citizens of any particular regime or followers of a distinctive way of life. Antony thus speaks of "Roman citizen[s]" only to efface the distinction between citizens and non-citizens, Romans and non-Romans, and he does so, moreover, precisely when he announces Caesar's private bequests to the people, emphasizes the direct, immediate relation between Caesar and his beneficiaries, and elevates Caesar to the supreme rank of "a Caesar." Telling the mutinous crowd they still do not know wherein "Caesar [has] thus deserv'd your loves," he discloses his will:

> Here is the will, and under Caesar's seal.
> To every Roman citizen he gives,
> To every several man, seventy-five drachmas.
>
> Moreover, he hath left you all his walks,
> His private arbours, and new-planted orchards,
> On this side Tiber; he hath left them you,
> And to your heirs for ever: common pleasures,
> To walk abroad and recreate yourselves.
> Here was a Caesar! when comes such another?
> (238–254)

Speaking, then, as a private man on a private occasion to other private men, Antony consistently suppresses the sort of manly strength Brutus emphasizes and emphasizes instead human weaknesses which Brutus omits. Where Brutus honors Caesar "for his valour," Antony celebrates him for caring most about the very things valor· disdains:

> When that the poor have cried, Caesar hath wept;
> Ambition should be made of sterner stuff.
> (93f.)²²

Caesar, he stresses, was ruled by a loving attachment to ordinary human needs and concerns. Glossing the sort of strength Caesar exults in before the Senate, he mentions, for example, the wealth he brought to Rome but never the martial prowess which won it. Similarly, when speaking of the "day he overcame the Nervii" (175), he stresses Caesar's mortality but says nothing about how "not a Roman [would have] escaped alive that day" "had not Caesar [him]self taken his shield on his arm, and flying in amongst the barbarous people, made a lane through them that fought before him."²³ And when describing his "mighty heart" (188), he emphasizes his butchered body and ruefully misplaced love, but neither his strengths nor his triumphs. Consistently overlooking Caesar's heroic virtue in the same way Caesar himself did when explaining his fall at the Lupercal, he suggests that Caesar refused the crown not out of respect for republican principles or tradition, but because he lacked the sense of manly strength that underlies and animates republicanism.

Antony refutes Brutus' charge by arguing in effect that Caesar could not have been ambitious because he loved and pitied the people. Because he was (and continues to be even in death) their greatest benefactor, he deserves their dearest love; and because he felt the deepest pity for them, he is worthy of their greatest pity. Antony's tacit premise is that ambition is incompatible with love

---

22. The part of Antony's speech expressly devoted to the charge of ambition (79–101) directly parallels the part of Brutus' speech bringing that charge (25–29). Brutus, defending the assassination, twice lists four things he gave Caesar; Antony, defending Caesar, offers a matching list of his own. The four items on his list correspond directly to the four on Brutus' list, but on the level of the people's real concerns.

For what is more likely to have brought tears to Caesar's eyes, see Plutarch, *Caesar,* 11.3.

23. *Ibid,* 20.3–5; *Shakespeare's Plutarch,* ed. W. W. Skeat (London: Macmillan and Co., 1875), 61.

and pity but inseparable from manly republican virtue. Thus, even as the people equate ambition as such with the ambition to become king, what they really fear is not monarchy but oppression by their proud class enemies. Owing to their literal-mindedness, they oppose Caesar's becoming their king; but owing to their fear of ambition, they welcome him as their protector. While "the corruption of the people is the key to the mastery of Rome,"[24] in the end that corruption is above all the willingness of Rome's great heroes to become the defenders of their class enemies. Whereas the people fear tyranny will arise from the undisguised pride of a Coriolanus, a comparison of *Caesar* and *Coriolanus* shows that it results from the feigned humility and kindness of a Caesar. The people open the door to tyranny when they no longer fear Rome's heroes, but, responding favorably to bribes and flattery, begin to regard them as their domestic defenders.[25]

Coriolanus, who would not stoop, did not conquer, while Caesar, who used the people's fear of ambition to conceal and advance his own ambition, became their god. Antony's impressive success thus rests decisively on his presenting Caesar as Caesar presented himself at the Lupercal. It rests on presenting him as a martyr rather than as a hero. For republican freedom, Shakespeare suggests, perishes where ambition can hide itself in the people's fear of ambition by parading as love and compassion for the poor.

3.

The ambiguity of Caesar's end stems largely from the fact that his death is at once the epitome and the antithesis of an heroic death and that Caesar intends it to be understood by opposite groups in these opposite ways. To the Senate and the old regime in general, he intends it to be seen as the culmination of Olympian greatness and strength; to the people and the new regime, as the martyrdom

---

24. Bloom, *Shakespeare's Politics*, 80.
25. See Machiavelli, *Discourses*, I.46, and Harvey C. Mansfield, Jr., *Machiavelli's New Modes and Orders* (Ithaca: Cornell Univ. Press, 1979), 142.

of a new sort of god.[26] Thus, on the one hand, Caesar strives to
embody perfectly all the traits of manliness. When confronted by
the "very dangerous" Cassius, he insists he is not liable to fear, "for
always I am Caesar" (I.ii.189–209). Similarly, when Calphurnia
urges him not to go to the Senate, he first claims absolute fearless-
ness and equanimity concerning death:

> Cowards die many times before their deaths;
> The valiant never taste of death but once.
> Of all the wonders that I yet have heard,
> It seems to me most strange that men should fear,
> Seeing that death, a necessary end,
> Will come when it will come.

and then goes so far as to claim superiority to Danger itself:

> Danger knows full well
> That Caesar is more dangerous than he.
> We are two lions litter'd in one day,
> And I the elder and more terrible.
> (II.ii.32–37; 44–47)

And, finally, in front of the Senate he goes still further, declaring his
absolute constancy and superiority to everything around him:

> I could be well mov'd, if I were as you;
> If I could pray to move, prayers would move me;
> But I am constant as the northern star,
> Of whose true-fix'd and resting quality
> There is no fellow in the firmament.
> The skies are painted with unnumber'd sparks,
> They are all fire, and every one doth shine;
> But there's but one in all doth hold his place.
> So in the world: 'tis furnish'd well with men,
> And men are flesh and blood, and apprehensive;
> Yet in the number I do know but one
> That unassailable holds on his rank,
> Unshak'd of motion; and that I am he,
> Let me a little show it, even in this,
> That I was constant Cimber should be banish'd
> And constant do remain to keep him so.
> (III.i.58–73)

---

26. Caesar "collaborates, as it were, in his own deification." Palmer, *Political Characters*, 37.

In front of the people, on the other hand, Caesar suppresses all such heroic claims to divinity and affects not just equality but even inferiority. To the one group his death is meant to show him as immovable as Mount Olympus and as constant as the northern star; to the other, as weak as the weakest mortal and as poor as the poorest man:

> But yesterday the word of Caesar might
> Have stood against the world; now lies he there,
> And none so poor to do him reverence.
> (III.ii.120–122)

Caesar's double-faced death is the direct result of Rome's new political situation. Caesar claims to be "in the world" what the northern star is in the sky. He claims to be a universal god. Rome's universal empire brings forth a "new heaven" as it establishes a "new earth" (*A&C* I.i.17). The gods of republican Rome were gods of the city. Essentially civic or public, they defended Rome's public good from the twin dangers of private corruption at home and military defeat abroad. They were emphatically worldly or political. Like the city they defended, which defined itself chiefly by opposition to enemies or outsiders, their worship was necessarily confined within a narrow or particular horizon. Their existence was inseparable from the primacy of the public realm. Universal empire, however, necessarily destroys that realm by obliterating the distinctness or particularity of Rome and, with it, the public realm which the old gods defended and upon which their existence and worship depended. Universal empire requires an universal god, but, as the success of Antony's funeral oration shows, an universal god is worshipped by private individuals, not by citizens. Its worship is personal because its horizon is universal. As universal empire destroys the separateness of a political community, it establishes the separateness of its individual members. Men are no longer primarily citizens. They are now first and foremost individuals, whose deepest concerns are essentially private and whose relation to their gods is therefore immediate and direct.[27]

---

27. See pp. 26–28, above.

As universal empire liberates private concerns, it diminishes the possibilities for genuine noble actions. Since actions derive their meaning largely from the causes they serve, the reduction of political causes to private causes deprives political life of its ennobling spirit and fundamentally alters the meaning of nobility.[28] Antony never urges the funeral crowd to admire "the noble Caesar" (III.ii.186) for his virtue *in* suffering, as Cominius, for example, honors the battle-scarred Coriolanus (*Cor*.II.ii.79ff.). Rather, following Caesar's own example at the Lupercal, he elicits pity *for* his suffering, making mutual pity and hence shared human suffering the principal sacred bond between Caesar and the people. By the same token, it is not despite but because his personal suffering makes him appear a "Poor soul" that the people can believe "There's not a nobler man in Rome than Antony." (III.ii.117f.). With the establishment of imperial Rome, nobility comes to be associated with human love and piteous suffering rather than with valiant actions and manly pride. Indeed, the one set of qualities led directly to the other: the appreciation of manly virtue to the celebration of universal love. Rome conquered the world by destroying the cities around her and readily accepting as citizens those she conquered so she could use them to conquer still more. To conquer everyone, Rome had to embrace everyone, so that her very conquests eventually transformed her basic principle of universal force into universal love.[29] It is therefore appropriate that Decius' interpretation of Calphurnia's dream alludes to Christian saints (II.ii.85–90), Antony's oration compares Caesar's "sacred blood" to that of Christian martyrs (III.ii.132–39), and Octavius alludes to the crucifixion of Jesus when speaking of Caesar's wounds (V.i.53).[30] Cassius indignantly insists that Caesar, although worshipped as a god, is no more than a pitiful mortal. Yet it is because of Rome's conquest of the world and Caesar's conquest of Rome that such a "man / Is now become a god" (I.ii.114f.). While Rome's universal empire,

---

28. See pp. 56–61, above.
29. Machiavelli, *Discourses*, II.3; Mansfield, *Machiavelli's New Modes and Orders*, 198.
30. See chapt. 3, n. 30 above.

reducing all men to private individuals, diminishes the glory of this world,[31] Caesar's death, at once an act of heroism and martyrdom, both connects and separates pagan and Christian, republican and imperial Rome. It begins the new as it completes the old.[32]

4.

Shakespeare's ambiguous presentation reflects the problematical relation between the old and the new Rome, and hence the dual character of Caesar's death and divinity. But it also demonstrates the political skills which enabled Caesar to reach the top in Rome. It reflects the means he used as well as the ends he pursued. We saw this in his manipulation of the people at the Lupercal. We see it again in his handling of Decius on the morning of the ides.

The scene with Decius (II.ii) is generally thought to show Caesar at his worst—superstitious, irresolute, arrogant and easily flattered. The keynote is struck at the end of the conspirators' meeting in the previous scene when Cassius warns,

> But it is doubtful yet
> Whether Caesar will come forth to-day or no;
> For he is superstitious grown of late,
> Quite from the main opinion he held once
> Of fantasy, of dreams, and ceremonies.
> It may be these apparent prodigies,
> The unaccustom'd terror of this night,
> And the persuasion of his augurers,
> May hold him from the Capitol to-day.

And Decius confidently assures him,

> Never fear that: if he be so resolv'd,
> I can o'ersay him; for he loves to hear

---

31. "It is a diminished world into which Shakespeare takes us after the death of Caesar." Palmer, *Political Characters*, 46. Rome has become Caesar's patrimony; cp. III.ii.249 with I.ii.152f.

32. That there may ultimately be something otherwordly about Coriolanus' isolating pride and uncompromising integrity is suggested by his last words to the Roman people: "Despising / For you the city, thus I turn my back. / There is a world elsewhere." (III.iii.133–135) The rest of his life shows that that other "world" is nowhere on earth.

> That unicorns may be betray'd with trees,
> And bears with glasses, elephants with holes,
> Lions with toils, and men with flatterers;
> But when I tell him he hates flatterers,
> He says he does, being then most flattered.
> Let me work;
> For I can give his humour the true bent,
> And I will bring him to the Capitol.
> (II.i.193–211)

Dreams and flattery indeed lie at the heart of the scene. As Caesar tells Decius that Calphurnia's dream keeps him from going to the Senate that day, so Decius' flattering reinterpretation of the dream apparently causes him to change his mind and go. Yet it is Caesar who, in telling the dream, gives Decius' ingratiating humor "the true bent," flattering him by letting him believe he can flatter Caesar, and, in so doing, induces him to betray his own purpose without his ever becoming aware that he has done so. The counterpart of the Lupercal scene, Caesar's exchange with Decius directly presents his political indirection. It shows him secretly defeating by openly gratifying his secret enemies.

As the scene begins, Caesar is awake despite the early hour. We know why the conspirators are up, but it is less clear why he should be. The violence and noise of the storm in the night and Calphurnia's cries in her sleep may have awakened him:

> Nor heaven nor earth have been at peace to-night:
> Thrice hath Calphurnia in her sleep cried out,
> "Help, ho! they murther Caesar!"
> (1–3)

But he may be awake for another reason as well. From what Casca tells Cicero, we learn that Caesar was with him, Antony and perhaps others during the night and that he intends to go to the Senate in the morning (I.iii.36–38). And, if only by rumor, Casca knows certain senators plan that day to make him king everywhere but in Italy:

> Indeed, they say the senators to-morrow
> Mean to establish Caesar as a king;

And he shall wear his crown by sea and land,
In every place, save here in Italy.
(I.iii.85–88)

Since Casca has heard this report, at best, secondhand, it would be
unreasonable to believe it could not have reached Caesar as well,
either through Casca, Antony, other senators, partisans, or spies.[33]
But if Caesar has heard the rumor, he must assume his very dangerous enemies such as Cassius have, too. Caesar nevertheless does
not send for a bodyguard or take any other precaution against
attack. Instead, he prepares to go to the Senate, as planned. When
Calphurnia enters and expresses fear for his safety, he first
dismisses her concern out of hand, but yields when she suggests a
pretext and begs on her knee. He yields to her fears just as Decius
arrives. While surely strengthening Caesar's suspicions, Decius'
unexpected arrival is not enough to confirm them or to indicate
where, when or how his assailants might attack. Caesar has no
reason to assume the republicans will make the mistakes they do.
For all he knows, they might strike him in the obscurity of his
home, use a furtive means such as poison, or even employ hired
agents. Caesar's yielding to Calphurnia thus gives him an
opportunity to test Decius' intentions. "And you are come in a very
happy time," he tells him,

To bear my greeting to the senators,
And tell them that I will not come to-day:
Cannot, is false; and that I dare not, falser;
I will not come to-day. Tell them so, Decius.
(60–64)

Caesar refuses to go or to explain why he will not go. But when
Decius asks for some cause, lest he be laughed at by the senators,
Caesar first reiterates his refusal—

The cause is in my will: I will not come;
That is enough to satisfy the Senate.

---

33. Caesar seems almost the only man in Rome ignorant of the plot against him. Popilius,
though not one of the conspirators, wishes them well (III.i.12ff.), and Artemidorus, a
foreign-born partisan of Caesar's, knows even of the last-minute inclusion of Ligarius
among the conspirators (II.iii.4).

—but then, expressly to gratify Decius, relates Calphurnia's dream and explains that she keeps him home because of it:

> But for your private satisfaction,
> Because I love you, I will let you know:
> Calphurnia here, my wife, stays me at home.
> She dreamt to-night she saw my statue,
> Which like a fountain with an hundred spouts
> Did run pure blood; and many lusty Romans
> Came smiling, and did bathe their hands in it.
> And these does she apply for warnings and portents
> And evils imminent; and on her knee
> Hath begg'd that I will stay at home to-day.

And Decius replies,

> This dream is all amiss interpreted;
> It is a vision fair and fortunate:
> Your statue spouting blood in many pipes,
> In which so many smiling Romans bath'd
> Signifies that from you great Rome shall suck
> Reviving blood, and that great men shall press
> For tinctures, stains, relics, and cognizance.
> This by Calphurnia's dream is signified.
> (71–90)

Caesar, though guarded, seems impressed by Decius' interpretation: "And this way have you well expounded it." (91) Decius, encouraged by this response, continues in his bid to make good on his boast to Cassius. He asserts that the interpretation refers to the Senate's (previously undisclosed) decision "To give this day a crown to mighty Caesar" (94),[34] and then, professing his "dear, dear love" (102), warns of what the senators might whisper about Caesar's courage were he to stay home because of his wife's bad dreams. Caesar, apparently swallowing it all, declares how foolish Calphurnia's fears now seem, expresses shame for having yielded to them, asks for his robe, and announces he will go.

---

34. Note that Decius omits the important limitation on the kingship that Casca mentions (I.iii.85–88).

While Caesar never looks more foolish than at this moment, he has learned everything he needs to know. As well as he knows how to interpret auspicies to suit his own purpose (37–48), he also knows how to present Decius with materials which he will interpret in such a way as unwittingly to divulge his own intentions. Contrary to first impressions, Caesar does not learn the details of her dream from Calphurnia. At the beginning of the scene, he says only that she thrice cried out in her sleep, "Help, ho! they murther Caesar!" and nothing in their conversation when she appears suggests they have spoken since she awoke. Calphurnia reminds Caesar of "the things that we have heard and seen" and reports in vivid detail the "most horrid sights seen by the watch," which she says frighten her (13–26), but does not mention her dream, and in fact never does. Calphurnia's dream is Caesar's fabrication. He attaches to the dream the interpretation she gave to the horrid sights, and thus replaces her explanation of her fears, and hence his reason for staying home, with one of his own.[35] The ruse works perfectly. In challenging the interpretation Caesar offers, Decius confirms the central facts. What was true of Caesar's statue in the dream will be true of Caesar himself in Rome—he will indeed spout blood like a fountain. Decius thus acknowledges that Calphurnia was correct in her "vision" and wrong only in judging whether Caesar's assassination will be good or bad. Only whether her "vision" was "fair and fortunate" was "amiss interpreted." No wonder Caesar tells him, "And this way have you well expounded it." Caesar has learned he will be slain that day and his murder will be what he wants—a bloody public spectacle in the Capitol.

The victory Decius imagines he has secretly won over Caesar is Caesar's real, secret victory over him. Once he hears Decius's words, Caesar never again wavers.[36] He greets the rest of the assassins with urbane provocations, reminding them of their debts to him as

---

35. Contrary to what Caesar implies, Calphurnia was frightened because the sights were so dreamlike and yet not a dream (13–26).
36. Michael Platt, *Rome and Romans According to Shakespeare* (Salzburg Studies in English Literature: *Institut für Englishe Sprache und Literatur*, 1976), 201.

well as their dependence, and when in public shows no concern whatever for what anyone could possibly give or take from him. Just as on the way to the Senate he displays indifference to what affects himself and concern for what affects others, so when he arrives in the Capitol he appropriates all giving (and even the Senate) to himself:

> What is now amiss
> That Caesar and his Senate must redress?
> (III.i.31f.)

From the moment he learns that he will be assassinated in a manner that will epitomize his life, Caesar acts like the god he claims to be.[37]

5.

Caesar does not aspire to be king but rather to force future kings to aspire to the rank of "Caesar." Unwilling to follow in the path of any established tradition, however illustrious, he seeks to found a new tradition in which his name is superior to any other honor and confers all legitimate title to rule. He intends to establish a Caesarian monarchy, but a monarchy in his name, not in his person.[38] Thus the cry of "Caesar" is fully audible to the partly deaf Caesar. Caesar, whose deafness is Shakespeare's invention, is in a sense deaf to everything but his name, and especially to the warning of danger (I.ii.12–24). His name, he claims, makes him more than a man by rendering him independent of fear:

> Would he were fatter! But I fear him not:
> Yet if my name were liable to fear,
> I do not know the man I should avoid
> So soon as that spare Cassius.

---

37. In Plutarch (*Caesar*, 66.4–5), Suetonius (*Divus Julius*, 82.1–2) and Appian (*The Civil Wars*, II.108), Caesar struggles with his killers. In Shakespeare, he does not.

38. *Non Rex sum sed Caesar* ("I am not king but Caesar."): Plutarch, *Caesar*, 60.2, Suetonius, *Divus Julius*, 79.2, Appian, *Civil Wars*, II.108. As Bloom (*Shakespeare's Politics*, 91) points out, Caesar's name did, of course, soon become synonymous with the grandest sort of monarchy. Beginning with Octavius (see III.i.276; V.i.24, 54, 57) and extending down to our own day, emperors have continued to rule as Caesars, Kaisers, Czars, and Shahs.

> I rather tell thee what is to be fear'd
> Than what I fear; for always I am Caesar.
> (I.ii.195–198,208f.)

Caesar's goal is to establish the divinity of "Caesar," to show that his name is the greatest power and to possess that name is to possess such power. "Would you praise Caesar, say 'Caesar,' go no further." (*A&C* III.ii.13) To be great, greatness will have to bear his name.

Caesar is ambitious for his name. He lives and dies for it. In this respect he is characteristically, if perversely, Roman. Coriolanus, who went to battle to "seek danger where he was like to find fame" (*Cor.* I.iii.12), not only derives his name from his defeated enemies, but somehow *is* what he is called. Without his name he is nobody.

> Coriolanus
> He would not answer to; forbade all names.
> He was a kind of nothing, titleless,
> Till he had forg'd himself a name i' th' fire
> Of burning Rome.
> (V.i.11–15)

Caesar and Coriolanus may seem exceptions, but they in fact typify the rule. It is often pointed out how frequently and grandiloquently Caesar refers to himself by name.[39] Nineteen times he calls himself "Caesar." Fittingly enough, his last word is his name: "Then fall Caesar!" (III.i.71) But Caesar is by no means alone in referring to himself in this manner. Brutus and Cassius do so more than a dozen times each, and even Casca does once, as does Portia. Moreover, all of these self-references occur in the context of either the characters' proudest Roman declarations or their most shameful defeats. They are all associated with manliness.[40] Cassius can there-

---

39. E.g., by MacCallum, *Shakespeare's Roman Plays*, 230f., Palmer, *Political Characters*, 36ff., and Platt, *Rome and Romans*, 203ff.

40. Brutus' most republican speech (II.i.46–58) is the only speech in the play beginning and ending with the speaker's own name; note in context I.iii.90, the only line of its sort in the play. It would be difficult to exaggerate the importance of names in *Caesar*. Despite the play's relative brevity, the names of leading characters are mentioned much more often in *Caesar* than in any other Shakespearean play. Whereas Hamlet's name occurs 85 times, Macbeth's 42, Othello's 34 and Lear's 15, Caesar's appears 229 times, Brutus' 144, Cassius' 75 and Antony's 70. Only *Antony and Cleopatra* comes close to *Caesar*.

fore draw Brutus into the conspiracy by invoking "the great opinion / That Rome holds of his name" (I.ii.315f.), and initially arouse him against Caesar by comparing the fates (and inherent qualities) of their names:

> Brutus and Caesar: what should be in that "Caesar"?
> Why should that name be sounded more than yours?
> Write them together, yours is as fair a name;
> Sound them, it doth become the mouth as well;
> Weigh them, it is as heavy; conjure with 'em,
> "Brutus" will start a spirit as soon as "Caesar".
> Now in the names of all the gods at once,
> Upon what meat doth this our Caesar feed,
> That he is grown so great? Age, thou art sham'd!
> Rome, thou hast lost the breed of noble bloods!
> When went there by an age, since the great flood,
> But it was fam'd with more than with one man?
> When could they say, till now, that talk'd of Rome,
> That her wide walks encompass'd but one man?
> Now is it Rome indeed, and room enough,
> When there is in it but one only man.
> O, you and I have heard our fathers say,
> There was a Brutus once that would have brook'd
> Th' eternal devil to keep his state in Rome
> As easily as a king.
> (I.ii.140–159)[41]

To Brutus, who vows he loves "The name of honour" more than he fears death (I.ii.88), as to other honor-loving Romans, names are most real. The name is the thing itself.

Caesar is hardly dead before his name is used as he intended. At his funeral the crowd urges that Brutus be the next Caesar, and Antony exclaims to them, "Here was a Caesar! when comes such another?" As Bloom remarks, Caesar's "own person would not have sufficed to this role; but the edifice carefully constructed by him *plus* the memory of his martyrdom formed an almost eternal imperium."[42] Caesar constructs the memory of his martyrdom, however, as carefully as the edifice of his Olympian grandeur. His

---

41. The ironic implication, we should note, is that Rome does indeed belong to "one man." Owing to Brutus' namesake, Rome belongs especially to him.
42. *Shakespeare's Politics,* 91.

death turns him into a god not only by saving him from the errors of humanity and its weaknesses, as Bloom argues, but also, or especially, by publicly demonstrating his human weakness and private suffering, as Antony shows. Caesar is not merely spared infamy by his murder; he is raised to the status of a god.

Shakespeare indicates both by what he omits from his historical sources and by what he adds to them that Caesar's actions are to be understood as having been undertaken with a view to his ambitious death. Unlike Plutarch and Suetonius, who discuss the numerous projects Caesar was planning at the time of his murder,[43] Shakespeare suppresses all his future plans for Rome[44] and avoids the impression that any were cut short by his death, but at the same time he invents his careful preparations for his assassination. According to the sources, Octavius was in Greece when he heard of Caesar's murder and only then decided to return to Rome.[45] In Shakespeare, "Caesar did write for him to come to Rome," and Octavius is "within seven leagues of Rome" at the time of the assassination and "is already come to Rome" before the end of the funeral (III.i.278ff.; III.ii.264ff.). It is important to note that neither Caesar's letters nor Octavius's arrival, both of which are wholly Shakespeare's inventions, serve any merely dramatic purpose. Octavius does not appear on stage until Act IV, scene i, which is to say, not for another year and a half. Only Caesar's preparations for the aftermath of his slaying require his heir's early return. And that the letters anticipate his killing is corroborated by three additional facts: the letters cause Octavius to act stealthily before the assassination; although written by Caesar, they direct Octavius not to Caesar but to Antony (and hence are not summonses for help); and Octavius' servant shows no surprise at hearing his master called "Octavius Caesar" (III.i.276ff.).[46]

---

43. Plutarch, *Caesar,* 58.2–5; Suetonius, *Divus Julius,* 44f.

44. One possible exception is I.iii.85–88, which some editors understand as a remote allusion to Caesar's planned expedition against the Parthians.

45. Plutarch, *Brutus,* 22.2, *Antony,* 16.1; Suetonius, *Divus Augustus,* 8.2; Appian, *Civil Wars,* III.9–11.

46. In addition, Antony knows exactly where to find Caesar's will.

While heightening the ambiguity and general sense of spiritual emptiness around him, Shakespeare's alterations also suggest that Caesar, having assured his preeminence among his rivals, has little to live for but much to die for. He is indeed "at the end of his career." Owing to his vast political accomplishments, there is no place left in the world for a man like him. If anyone in the Roman plays is interested in the sort of enterprises Plutarch says he planned, it is not Caesar but his successors (*A&C* II.vii.17ff.). As Bloom notes, "One can hardly imagine that such a man could settle down to the career of a peaceful public administrator."[47] Nor would Caesar be content, like some later Caesars, to use his political position to indulge his private lusts. Caesar's achievements may have destroyed the ancient political world, but he remains a completely political man to the end, seeking immortal fame and glory, not bodily pleasure. His passions and aims are personal only in the sense that he seeks a political victory that is entirely his own, one in which what is personally his replaces what belongs to the city as such. There is nothing hedonistic or private about this Caesar. Even in private with his wife, he lacks privacy. Caesar could, of course, seek to become a living god. Indeed, Cassius says he is already on his way to becoming one (I.ii.114ff.). But, as Caesar's last appearance in the Capitol vividly demonstrates and as Shakespeare's apparently unfavorable presentation of him generally suggests, there is no way to distinguish genuine praise and love from the mere flattery and fear of a man who dominates the world and in whom all obedience and giving are concentrated.

But Caesar looks forward to death not so much because life holds no more conquests for him as because death alone promises him his true crowning conquest. Fulfilling his ambition to recreate Rome in his own image, it allows him to set a single goal for ambitious men beyond their reach—to be Caesar—while at the same time establishing himself as a new sort of god—one that is universal, above political rule, possessing and inspiring a sort of

---

47. *Shakespeare's Politics*, 90.

strength that is thought to be superior to manliness and inseparable from pity, and directly and immediately related to its worshippers. Combining reverence based on pity or love with reverence based on awe, Caesar's double-faced death, epitomizing both his political and military lives, brings together the sublime remoteness of "the northern star" and the personal closeness of "sweet Caesar's wounds" (III.ii.227) and "sacred blood." Caesar therefore goes to his death not only knowingly but willingly. Indeed, he goes to it in some sense like a traditional Roman—"pleas'd to . . . seek danger where he was like to find fame."

Yet, as Shakespeare presents it, Caesar's lasting achievement, like his death on the one hand and Brutus' problematical virtue on the other, seems ultimately more melancholic than glorious. It diminishes men's hearts as it expands their horizons and, by depriving them of opportunities for noble actions and triumphs in this world, forces them finally to seek glory and salvation in the next. In Titinius' words, "The sun of Rome is set. Our day is gone; / . . . our deeds are done." (V.iii.63f.) There are no worldly causes left worthy enough to fight for. Caesar's own victory, however, shares this unhappy fate. The fulfillment of Roman ambition necessarily comes too late, for it can come only at the end of the Republic's decline and not at the peak of its strength. Caesar's triumph—the end of the Republic which reveals its true beginnings—presupposes the corruption, as it implies the destruction, of republican Rome. Caesar's glory is therefore in some sense hollow or vain, though in another sense immortal. It is inseparable from a diminution of the hearts of men and an accompanying disillusionment or disenchantment with the beauty of this world. The world can no longer seem "majestic" to men who must live in Caesar's shadow (see esp. I.ii.91–136). Caesar claims to be in the world what the northern star is in the sky. But the northern star, as Caesar seems to forget, is visible only at night. It may indeed display an unrivaled "true-fix'd and resting quality," but its quality and glory stand out only against a darkened sky.

INDEX